July 2014-OOP
Sept 2015-OOP
Nov 2019-OOP

5 Cdn.

D0098899

GOING THE DISTANCE

7 STEPS TO PERSONAL CHANGE

RICK HANSEN

AND

DR. JOAN LAUB

DOUGLAS & MCINTYRE
Vancouver/Toronto

Douglas & McIntyre Ltd.
1615 Venables Street
Vancouver, British Columbia
V5L 2H1

The publisher gratefully acknowledges the assistance of the Canada Council and of the British Columbia Ministry of Tourism, Small Business and Culture for its publishing programs.

Canadian Cataloguing in Publication Data

Hansen, Rick, 1957-
  Going the distance

  ISBN 1-55054-119-6

  1. Personality change. 2. Change (Psychology). 3. Self-realization. 4. Personality and motivation. I. Laub, H. Joan (Helen Joan), 1954- II. Title.
BF698.2.H36 1994   158'.1   C94-910471-X

Editing by Brian Scrivener
Text design by George Vaitkunas
Jacket Design by Tom Brown
Printed and bound in Canada by D.W. Friesen & Sons Ltd.
Printed on acid-free paper ∞

CONTENTS

Foreword   iv

Preface   viii

Acknowledgements   ix

Introduction   1

How to Use This Book   2

Guiding Philosophy   4

The Process of Personal Change: An Overview   10

Preparing for Change   15

Step #1. **Setting Your Goal**   **25**

Step #2. **Cultivating Your Personal Vision**   **41**

Step #3. **Planning to Reach Your Goal**   **49**

Step #4. **Taking Risks**   **69**

Step #5. **Embracing Feelings**   **89**

Step #6. **Actively Striving**   **109**

Step #7. **Experiencing Success**   **135**

Troubleshooting   151

Re-Orientation Toward Living   159

Afterword   177

Index   179

FOREWORD

Often, people ask me if I would exchange the life I have led since my accident for the use of my legs. Sometimes they seem shocked or disbelieving when I invariably answer, "No."

As do most kids at age fifteen, I thought I had the world by the tail on June 27, 1973. I had just received athlete-of-the-year honours at my high school and was looking forward to trying out for the provincial volleyball team later in the summer. It was a great life. It was a beautiful day. My friend Don and I were hitchhiking back home from doing a little fishing—even that had been good—and we hoped to get back to Williams Lake in time to watch a local rodeo.

After a while, we caught a ride with a guy and his girlfriend in a pickup. Somehow in my gut I knew it was a mistake—the guy was knocking back a beer as he invited us to hop in. We jumped in the back and the driver headed out along the gravel road toward Williams Lake. It was a long and bumpy trip. Don and I took turns trying to keep the box of fish we'd caught from bouncing out of the truck. We also tried to get a little rest. I had dozed off but was suddenly awakened by a scream and the swerving of the vehicle. I remember looking up and seeing that we were skidding out of control. I glanced quickly at Don; his eyes were as big as saucers. I knew that we were in trouble and was immediately overwhelmed by fear.

The truck lurched from side to side and finally overturned. Don was thrown clear and was relatively unhurt. I was not so lucky. The large, steel toolbox that I had been lying on in the back of the truck was pitched out as we overturned. I landed full force on the edge of the box. My back snapped like a twig, and I lost consciousness. When I came to a few moments later, I knew that I would live, and instantly wished that I wouldn't.

I lay crumpled against the box, covered with debris. When I tried to move a searing pain raged through my back, blotting out everything except the thought that I wasn't moving. Something was dreadfully wrong. A cold, sick feeling grew deep in my stomach as I realized that my legs weren't working. I sent the messages, but they didn't respond. They just lay there numb, like jelly, like they were dead. Fear and dread came at me. I was still fifteen, but I wasn't a kid any more.

Deep inside a little voice was telling me that this was serious, very serious. I tried to hold that voice at bay with logic and optimism. Hey, I'd been injured before and had gotten better—how bad could it be? Yes, another voice said, but this time it was going to be different.

I lay there for an hour fighting the pain and fear, and losing. The ambulance arrived and took me to Williams Lake Hospital. There I received emergency treatment for my injuries, and then, that afternoon, the doctors came in with my X-rays. They told me that I would never walk again. I was torn between disbelief and despair. To never walk again, never run, never do anything. Being alive seemed little consolation.

The doctors decided that I should be transferred to the Royal Columbian Hospital in New Westminster for surgery. The operation repaired whatever could be done and for the next two months I lay in a Stryker Frame. The Stryker Frame is uncomfortable, but ingenious in its simplicity. It's basically a hard, narrow bed pad set in the middle of a large, circular metal framework. Initially, I was placed within the frame on my stomach. After being in that position for a few hours, another hard, narrow bed pad was laid on my back and bolted in tight. Then the whole thing was rotated 180 degrees and the top bed pad was removed. Voilà! I was now lying on my back. This went on every three hours for weeks at a time.

Late one evening I began to feel nauseous and finally vomited about 3 a.m. Fortunately, I was at least in the face-down position, the bed pad supporting my forehead and a cut-out area of the pad framing my face. I called for the duty nurse, but for some reason, no one came for hours. I stared down at what had been my evening meal as the fever continued to ravage my body. I lay there sweating, head pounding, my back on fire with pain. The stench below me wafted up from the floor. I was unable to move. I was alone, and perhaps for the first time in my life, absolutely helpless. A wave of anxiety crashed over me, bigger and heavier than the ones before . . . bigger and heavier than all the ones before combined. I began to shake in utter despair and cried on into the night.

At that moment I wanted everything to be over. At that moment my life seemed worthless. Nothing I was doing was working. I felt helpless and out of control, and the thought of spending the rest of my life in a wheelchair brought with it visions of unending depression, dependence and confinement. I hoped that it was just a bad dream, that I would wake up and be alright.

It's been about twenty years since that desperate night. How could I have known that I would be able to look back over my life from this vantage point with such a great sense of fulfilment and contentment? It would have been impossible to convince that scared kid lying there in the dark that he would eventually have a wonderful wife and children, a successful career in business and the legacy of the Man In Motion World Tour. He could not have imagined that he would eventually come to be excited and optimistic about his future.

Yet, it is true. How did it happen? Of course I feel fortunate that I was given the chance to bring out the best in myself, but how can others learn from what I have gone through? How was I able to overcome the barriers, both internal and external? These are the questions that motivated me to begin the journey that culminated in this book.

There is no doubt in my mind that the following steps, principles and strategies have made a difference in my life, and I am sure that they can be applied to your life as well. Whether your personal change goals are big or small, whether you come from the country or the city, whether you are a business person, public employee, millworker, homemaker or student, this book offers something to all who have the desire to make change happen for them. In it, my experience is presented as a metaphor to illustrate the attitude, perspective and skills I have found useful in making life changes. I hope that *Going the Distance* will be a beacon of light to guide you through the change process, allowing you to embrace change and work more effectively as you strive to achieve your own success.

Rick Hansen

PREFACE

My involvement in this book originates from a two-year research project on personal transformation that I completed in 1991 at the University of British Columbia. My motivation and interest for this research were rooted in the fact that helping people change is what I do for a living. However, my training and experience as a psychologist notwithstanding, I believe that people are capable of accomplishing personal change without the help of a professional.

In my quest to understand how people change, I soon learned that, strangely enough, very little research had been done on how people actually accomplish personal change. Instead, most of the research focused on *what* and *why* people change, not on *how* they do it. So, I set out to assemble and study real-life accounts of personal transformation. Rick was among those who agreed to participate in my study.

My overall aim was to identify how *diverse* individuals accomplished personal change and what, if anything, they had in common. Through an intensive analysis of the data, I discovered consistent principles woven throughout all the individual accounts of change. Second, and most importantly, I found there was an overarching process of change common to all the accounts. These findings were distilled from the research and are summarized within this book.

After the project was completed, Rick approached me about the possibility of collaborating on a book about personal change, a passion and interest we both shared. Over the course of the research study we had enjoyed working together, so it was only natural that we join together again in a project of mutual interest.

Joan Laub

ACKNOWLEDGEMENTS

I would like to dedicate this book to my wife, Amanda. It has been through her consistent encouragement, friendship and love that I have been able to have the courage to look in the mirror and see what I am, be challenged to look toward the future and see what I can be, and strive to achieve that vision regardless of how I feel.

Many thanks, obviously, go to my friend, colleague and co-author, Joan Laub, for believing in the possibilities of this book, for her incredible contribution to it and, most importantly, for 'going the distance'.

I would also like to acknowledge the outstanding contribution of our editor and spiritual co-author Brian Scrivener, who went beyond the call of duty. Thank you to Miranda, Taanta, Flora, Edie and the countless other team members who helped turn this dream into a reality.

RH

Heartfelt gratitude flows out to my co-conspirator Gary Alexander who "fathered" this book. In his typical selfless fashion, he willingly and generously shared with me his talent, knowledge and experience as a writer. His presence shines like a light through every page. I realize my good fortune to have crossed paths with this wise, old soul; he has changed my perspective deeply, profoundly and forever.

I also want to thank my mentor, Dr. Larry Cochran. His unwavering search for truth and what matters has been a major driving force in my professional development. In his ongoing contribution to my search, he offered his expert guidance and commented cogently on this manuscript. His laser-like mind and discerning eye always helps me cut through the fog.

My sincere appreciation goes to the following people who helped and supported me in many ways:

To my friend, Carolyn Robertsen, for her steadfast loyalty and for all those late-night conversations that sustained my sanity.

To Brian Scrivener for his editorial input, his humour and his seasoned perspective. I also want to acknowledge his significant effort to shepherd this book through its final phases.

And, to Miranda Sharpe for her diligence and diplomacy, as well as her willingness to do anything she could to make the impact of the distance between me and everyone else a great deal easier.

Finally, I want to thank Rick for making this project possible. His courage is truly inspirational and his openness is delightfully refreshing. I am truly grateful for having had the opportunity to touch minds with a person of his calibre.

JL

INTRODUCTION

The aim of this book is to share what we have learned about personal change with as wide an audience as possible. We want to emphasize at the outset that we don't offer any definitive answers, nor do we offer a quick-fix approach.

What we do offer is a **unique blend** of general principles and practical strategies based on scholarly research and concrete personal experience. Most importantly, we offer an overall framework to guide you through the process of personal change.

The general principles from our individual experiences have been combined with numerous strategies useful in facilitating the process of change. Through the spirit of collaboration and the tremendous synergy that resulted we have created a new and exciting approach to personal change.

The result is this book. We believe that *Going the Distance* will take you step-by-step through an innovative process of personal change that can be effectively and readily applied to anyone's life.

How to Use This Book

Virtually anyone interested in personal change can use this book. Regardless of who you are, what you do or how many problems you believe you have, you can use this book and benefit from the application of its principles and strategies. Our intention is not to lead you through a complete personal overhaul. *Going the Distance* will work for you without a professional advisor, a guru or years of counselling. If you read the book carefully and make a sincere, wholehearted effort to apply the principles and strategies it contains, you will reap the benefits. If you commit yourself to studying and completing this process you will be empowered to live in a more meaningful, productive and fulfilling way.

By selecting this book, it is clear you are seeking or at least you are interested in personal change. Some of you may desire change, but feel blocked. If you need assistance, a little or a lot, this book provides straightforward guidance and direction. It offers practical, easy-to-follow steps for achieving self-directed personal change. You can apply this process to any endeavour, whether it be personal effectiveness, business success or improved athletic performance.

To make the best use of this book, read or at least scan its entirety to get a sense of the process as a whole. Next, read the book again with a focus on its principles or individual parts. Then, return to Step #1 and persevere, step-by-step, through the process. Specific strategies are included in each chapter to guide you. We recommend that you keep a journal for jotting down answers to questions, ideas and insights, as well as significant thoughts and feelings that arise as you work your way through the change process.

Keep in mind that there is no one right way to use this book. Each person is unique, an original. Although the basic structure of the change process is the same for everybody, each of us experiences the process differently. You can use this book most effectively as a guide or a framework for your own change process. Ultimately, your journey toward personal change will follow a course that can be led by no one else but you.

GUIDING PHILOSOPHY

You probably haven't sat down and really thought much about the concept of human development. But, in order to fully understand and benefit from the material presented in this book, it is necessary to address this topic, at least briefly. The reason it is so important is this. We all adhere to some model of human development, but usually we don't make our perspective explicit. Yet, it is our perspective on human development, whether we are conscious of it or not, that guides and directs our thoughts, feelings and actions about our capacity for personal change. For this reason, it is useful to review the main models of human development to help you identify which one best reflects your current perspective.

Essentially, there are three main models of human development: the **reactive** model, the **active** model and the **interactive** model. For the sake of brevity, we will summarize only the core of each perspective.

Advocates of the **reactive** model understand human beings as essentially passive in their own development. Human development is viewed as the result of external or environmental forces which act on individuals and to which individuals react. People grow to be what they are because of their respective environments and circumstances. If you adhere to this model, you believe that change is the result of environmental influences and external forces. People don't make change happen, they merely react to the changes that happen to them.

Supporters of the **active** model understand people as active agents in their own development. Development is viewed as the result of internal forces within the individual. External or environmental events are not viewed as determining forces of development. People grow to be what they are because of the forces within them. If you adhere to this model, you believe that people make change happen and the role of the environment or external forces in creating change is relatively insignificant.

Advocates of the **interactive** model incorporate aspects of both the reactive and active models. They understand people as active agents who play a role in their own development and who, at the same time, are influenced by external forces. Development is viewed as the result of an actively changing individual within the context of an actively changing environment. People, then, are in a state of constant change originating both within and without. If you adhere to this model, you believe that people are capable of making change happen, as well as of having change happen to them.

Our philosophy of human development fits within the interactive model. We believe that people play a role in their own development, while, at the same time, they are influenced by environmental forces. On the basis of this philosophy, we conclude that people have the capacity to be active rather than passive in shaping the course of their lives. We also believe that people must learn to respond effectively to the external influences that inevitably arise.

With these three models of human development in mind, can you identify which of them most accurately reflects your current perspective? If you find yourself aligned with a model different from ours, don't worry. The main point here is to be aware of your present perspective. By the time you complete our process of personal change, you will more than likely find yourself re-evaluating your position.

Our Philosophy of Change

Heraclitus, the Greek philosopher, reminded us that we cannot step twice into the same river, for other waters are continually flowing in. He was also the one who said that there is nothing as permanent as change. In one form or another, we have all heard it before: change is a part of life.

This inescapable truth validates the significance of change. Change affects all of us, all of the time. We are well aware that our world is constantly changing, at an ever-increasing rate. As well, each of us is also in a state of constant change—mentally, emotionally, physically and spiritually. The way in which we experience change, however, can be either positive or negative, depending upon our response to it.

Based on our philosophy of human development, we believe that there are choices available to us about how we respond to change. This ability, this freedom to choose our responses, is one of the distinctly human capabilities that differentiates us from all other animals.

We see four possible responses to change:

First, we can be **inactive**. We can withdraw from change and do nothing. This response is reminiscent of the phenomenon of learned helplessness, a term coined by the psychologist Martin Seligman to describe people who, based on their mistaken belief that responding doesn't make a difference, just give up trying altogether.

Second, we can be **reactive**. This response involves reacting to change that arises externally in our environments. There is no choice involved—we merely react to change, like puppets on strings.

The third way is to be **proactive**. This approach involves choosing our response to change. We make informed choices and act in accordance with those decisions. Through the exercise of choice, we constructively respond to change and effectively incorporate it into our lives.

A fourth way is to be a **self-directed initiator** of change. This approach involves not only effectively managing change but also embracing and initiating change. People who embrace change view it as an opportunity for personal development and, therefore, actively initiate it. Adhering to this perspective allows us to influence and actively shape the course of our lives while effectively managing those changes that happen to us.

So, these are our choices. We can avoid or react to change, or we can manage it constructively. We can be victims of change, or we can embrace change. Because our philosophy is based on the belief that people both make things happen and have things happen to them, our choice is to learn to manage change effectively and, at the same time, be self-directed initiators of change. Exercising this uniquely human capacity enables us to take charge of our lives and helps us live in more productive and personally meaningful ways.

According to Richard deCharms, a prominent researcher in the field of motivation, the *primary human motivation* is to be effective in producing changes in one's environment. Exercising this capacity allows us to feel that we control or at least can influence our fate. By being active rather than passive, we come to feel powerful rather than powerless. Similarly, Julian Rotter, another psychologist and researcher, suggests that people feel differently depending upon whether they believe that their fate is under internal or external control. "Internal" people expect that what they want is determined by personal effort, ability and initiative. "External" people expect that what they want is determined by other people, social structures, luck or fate. Internals feel in charge of what happens in their lives, whereas externals feel helpless, at the mercy of the things and people around them.

Given our belief that human beings have the capacity to effectively manage as well as to initiate change, we are making the following three fundamental assumptions:

Assumption #1

It is better to exercise this basic capacity than not to. To us, exercising this capability is vital to our healthy functioning as we seek to optimize life's opportunities and manage life's challenges. This perspective has been linked to a number of general indicators of healthy functioning such as goal-achievement, emotional adjustment, self-esteem, physical health, problem-solving ability, quality of social relationships, vitality and life satisfaction.

Assumption #2

This ability is learned, not innate. Therefore, those who want to learn how to develop or to enhance this ability have that choice.

Assumption #3

The experience of effectively managing and initiating change is a positive one that is extremely rewarding and satisfying. People who embrace change reap enormous benefits, including a sense of personal fulfilment and meaningfulness.

So, if change is so valuable and feels so good, why do so many people have so much trouble dealing with it? People generally fear and resist change because it involves the unknown. After all, it is also human nature to be more comfortable with what is familiar and predictable. If we avoid change, we maintain a certain level of comfort. Unfortunately, the cost is that we maintain a status quo which is not always very satisfying or fulfilling.

From our perspective, the problem is frequently one of lacking the good old-fashioned know-how—the knowledge, skills and strategies needed to manage change effectively. Therefore, one of our primary objectives is to provide this know-how in an effort to help you enhance your basic ability to manage and, ultimately, to learn to comfortably initiate change.

THE PROCESS
OF PERSONAL CHANGE:
AN OVERVIEW

There has been a longstanding interest in the subject of personal change. Historically, it has been resurrected under a variety of names and presented from a variety of perspectives. Over the last decade, the public has been offered a bewildering array of self-help books that give advice on how to achieve an assortment of goals: how to be successful, how to be effective, how to gain mastery over your life, how to get rich, how to achieve happiness, how to be an optimist or how to be all you can be. Despite the diversity of labels and perspectives, the basic underlying phenomenon in all these examples is *how people achieve personal change.*

What we all have gained from the self-help movement are many valuable insights about individual aspects of successful personal change. However, what seems to have happened is that we have ended up with an impressive collection of isolated parts. What has been missing is information about how these parts fit together as a whole—in other words, the overall **process** that is involved in achieving personal change.

Our intention in this book is to provide you with a beginning framework for understanding that process. We want to emphasize that what we are offering is a means to many different ends. You can apply this process to virtually any goal. Our purpose is not to determine your goal, but rather to help you understand a way by which you can

---

* Readers interested in a more theoretical perspective on the change process
can refer to *Becoming an Agent: Patterns and Dynamics for Shaping Your Life,*
co-authored by Dr. Larry Cochran and Dr. Joan Laub.

reach your own self-defined goals more effectively. The ultimate outcome, as we see it, is not merely success in reaching your goal. It is the cultivation of your ability, and faith in your ability, to achieve self-directed change, however you choose to define it.

What You Need to Know Before You Start

Before taking the first step, you should be aware that the process of personal change is cyclic. It is neither steady nor sudden; rather, it swings up and down. The size and intensity of these cycles vary with the individual. Cycles up tend to reflect the positive experiences or progression, while cycles down reflect the negative experiences or regression (setbacks). Each cycle, whether up or down, whether it feels good or bad, is vital in helping you move forward in the process.

This information is valuable for a number of reasons. With it, you can anticipate having periods of ups and downs, progress and setbacks, as you work your way through the change process. You can anticipate the cycles down and recognize them as inevitable and necessary parts of the process, not as discouraging failures. Knowing this in advance can help decrease your anxiety when you do encounter setbacks. It also helps to keep your expectations realistic, so that you don't expect smooth sailing at all times.

Below is a graph to illustrate the cyclic nature of the change process as we know it. The straight, diagonal line is the objective change-line. It reflects what is done, the actions taken. It moves steadily upward because each step involves new learning, and it is therefore additive, representing progress forward. The wavy line is the subjective change-line. It is cyclic and reflects the emotional highs and lows that are inevitably experienced over the course of a personal change.

Change-Lines

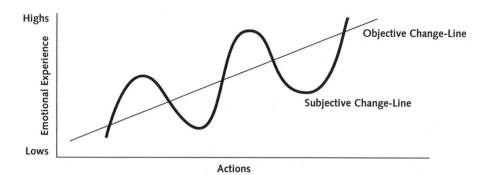

The 7 Steps to Personal Change

Since we are presenting a step-by-step process of personal change, a cautionary word about the organization and presentation of the steps is called for. While, based on the research, there does appear to be some sequential necessity to the ordering of the steps, there is no absolute or right order. That is, some steps naturally precede others because they set the stage for the next step. Other steps naturally flow from the cumulative effect of previous steps. However, there is no exact point at which one step starts and the other ends. Rather, they tend to overlap and blend together.

The seven steps to personal change are these:

Step #1

Setting your goal

This step involves identifying a meaningful personal change goal.

Step #2

Cultivating your personal vision

This step involves creating a personal vision of your goal using all your senses.

Step #3

Planning to reach your goal

This step involves designing a realistic action plan to attain your goal.

Step #4

Taking risks

This step involves initiating the action plan. Any action directed toward reaching your goal is defined as a risk because it entails new behaviour and facing the unknown.

Step #5

Embracing feelings

As you take action, powerful feelings will inevitably arise. This step involves finding a direct and constructive means of expression for these feelings rather than avoiding or ignoring them.

Step #6

Actively striving

This step involves sustaining the action required to attain your goal and addressing the obstacles that naturally arise along the way.

Step #7

Experiencing success

Through the cumulative effect of the preceding steps, you eventually achieve an experience of success. The experience is marked by a culminating event which signals attainment of the goal and provides a sense of completion.

What You Get When You Finish

Through the experience of initiating, sustaining and completing the process, you will achieve your goal. You will also change and develop in other significant ways. You will gain a boost in your self-confidence as a result of your experience of success. By pursuing a goal based on an authentic, meaningful motive, you will clarify which life activities matter to you. By actively participating with the world in a more meaning-ful way, you may clarify a broader sense of purpose and direction. Through achieving self-directed change, you will also learn about taking personal responsibility for influencing and shaping the course of your life. The cumulative effect of the process is a re-orientation toward life's possibilities. You will have cultivated an awareness of and a faith in your ability to effectively manage and initiate change. With increased confidence and vitality, you will see a future rich with possibility and be motivated to begin the process of change once again.

Preparing for Change

Returning home to Vancouver after completing the Man In Motion World Tour was an incredible experience. The dream that I had nurtured for years was finally becoming a reality and, in the end, it was just as I imagined it. When your dream and reality meet and become one, well, it's hard to describe. It's a deeply personal, almost singular feeling. Others might imagine it, but only you can know it. During the tour I felt that we were touching the hearts of millions of people. But, once we had finished, once we were back home, I was positive that our message of awareness and hope about the potential of people with disabilities rang clear. And people around the world had converted their feelings into action: they had given $26 million for spinal cord injury research.

Man, were we justified in celebrating! We did, but a couple of heady months after the tour, I suddenly found myself feeling empty and incomplete. What was this all about? Wasn't the tour the be-all, the end-all for Rick Hansen? Hadn't I done what no one else had done? Gone where no one else had gone before? Wasn't it enough? Apparently not. That was the old Rick Hansen talking. It was quickly obvious to me that I was not going to reap a lifetime of contentment and fulfilment from a single accomplishment. Clearly, I didn't have the answer—I had another question: "Where do I go from here?"

The new Rick Hansen had to begin sorting things out from the perspective he'd gained on the tour. I began to realize how profoundly the tour and the last two years had changed me. It was finally clear to me that I had to spend time getting in touch with myself, reviewing what I believed in, what was important to me and why. I was going to have to select new goals, and those goals were going to have to be based on who I was at that moment, not who I had been two years before. That didn't mean that I had to lock myself up in a monastery and meditate until I became enlightened. It simply meant that I had to take a little time to think about who I was now and what made me happy.

So with this awkward beginning, so reminiscent of how I had felt when I had begun the tour, I set off on another journey, one of self-discovery. Although, at first, I didn't have a specific goal in mind, somehow I knew I was starting over and would have to apply the same principles. In those months after the tour, I found myself continuing to search the past for guidance. I began to think about exactly how I had accomplished my part in the Man In Motion World Tour. I started to see familiar patterns emerging time after time. It was clear that there were common principles at work and that the topic of change was indeed becoming a goal in itself.

•

In order to be able to identify a worthwhile personal change goal, you will need to sharpen your awareness about yourself. By awareness, we mean accurately describing yourself to yourself, particularly in terms of your unique thoughts, feelings, interests and aspirations. Essentially, sharpening awareness is a process of getting better acquainted with yourself. Without a sense of *who* you are and *what* or *where* you want your life to be, self-directed change is next to impossible. Without this knowledge, we tend to react more than act. An aware person is in a better position to decide, to plan and to take self-directed action.

There's an old Sufi tale that sheds light on what we mean. A man who had studied at many metaphysical schools came to the great teacher Nasrudin. To show that he should be accepted as a disciple, he described in detail where he had been and what he had studied. "I hope that you will accept me, or at least tell me your ideas," he said, "because I have spent so much of my time studying at these schools." "Alas!" said Nasrudin, "you have studied the teachers and their teachings. What should have happened is that the teachers and the teachings should have studied you. Then we would have something worthwhile."

The following strategies are designed to help you 'study yourself' and sharpen your awareness.

Strategy: Keeping a Journal

As we mentioned in the How to Use This Book section, we recommend that you keep a journal. Your journal will be a place to record answers to the questions we pose, along with your thoughts and feelings, insights and ideas. It provides an opportunity for reflection and gathers into one place an ongoing commentary on what you have done and how you have felt about it.

Keeping a journal is also a way of recording your progress, a road map of your movement along the route to your goal. When we ask you later to review and identify key features that contributed to your success, you will have a written account of what happened. As well, if you encounter difficulties along the way, you will be better able to pinpoint the problem if you can refer to your journal and see where you might have gone off track.

There are no particular rules for keeping a journal. Develop your own style. Try not to place value judgements on what you are recording, and try to write without self-censorship. Don't restrict yourself—anything goes! For example, you may want to include meaningful quotes or sayings that inspire you, or you may find it easier to draw rather than write about what you are experiencing. You may want to use different coloured pens to communicate different thoughts or feelings, or to accentuate a significant point. Work in whatever medium feels most comfortable for you.

To begin your journal, jot down in a notebook any thoughts or feelings you may have right now about beginning the change process.

Strategy: Drawing Your Personal Development Line

Using a line graph like the one shown below, draw a line that shows the past, present and future of your personal development. Where have you been? Where are you now? Where do you want to be in the future? Mark important decision points with an X and label them.

Rick's Personal Development Line

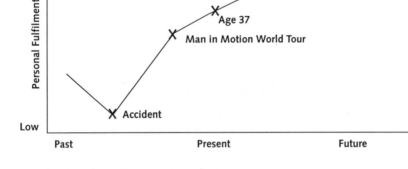

Your Personal Development Line

Is your line straight? Or does the line move upward or downward? Given what you see, do you feel you have fulfilled your potential? Are you satisfied with *who* you are and *where* you are? Is there a gap between who you are and who you want to be? Or, is there a gap between where you are and where you want to be? Pay special attention to your future hopes. Whom do you want to be in the future? Where do you want to be in the future? Record important thoughts and feelings in your journal.

Now, based on your answers to these questions, identify some things that you want to improve, develop or change about yourself.

Here are some that Rick identified for himself recently:

- Be a better father.
- Be a better husband.
- Achieve a better balance between my personal and professional lives.
- Explore new ways to contribute to the lives of others.
- Explore my spiritual side.

Strategy: Identifying Role Models

Another way you can sharpen awareness is by paying attention to potential role models. Role models are people whom we can emulate to good advantage. In order to be helpful, though, role models should be people whom you respect and admire. They should also represent or stand for something that is personally meaningful to you. As well, you should be able to identify with them in a way that you can apply to the task at hand.

Role models can be extremely valuable because they can reveal the range of possibilities. They can show you new ways of being, and provide you with new perspectives. They can also offer inspiration and motivation. In some or all of these ways, they can help you increase and clarify your awareness of potential goals.

As you think about potential role models, it is important to pay attention to both the positive and the negative ones. That is, consider role models you hope to emulate as well as those you will try your best to avoid.

●

After the truck accident, I was temporarily moved to a geriatric ward while waiting to go to a rehabilitation centre. There was an older paraplegic on the ward who was being treated for bed sores. He drank all the time, a broken man who seemed to make it through life by staying drunk. This was the first role model of a paraplegic that I had an opportunity to observe; I was repulsed. "No way," I thought, "I'm not going to be like this guy." The image of this man remained in the back of my mind as I set my goals, a negative model of one possible future that I must avoid at all costs.

In the spring of 1975, not long after my accident, I was out of the hospital and back in high school, but I was still having trouble adjusting. I felt sorry for myself and was quite depressed. As I headed toward class one day, a man came alongside me in his red convertible. "I hear that you were a good athlete. I also hear that you play table tennis and other sports. Why not come down to Vancouver and get in a little competition?" He had his wheelchair in the back seat and a Canadian Paraplegic Association decal on his windshield.

That's how I met Stan Stronge, one of the true pioneers in wheelchair sports, and a man who became a life-long friend. Stan was paralyzed in 1940—a time when people with spinal injuries seldom survived. He was driving through a heavy November storm when a tree fell on his car, paralyzing him from the chest down. Just recently married, Stan was a month shy of his thirtieth birthday. He spent a long time in the hospital and was discharged on a Sunday—December 7, 1941— the day Pearl Harbor was bombed. In those days there was no Paraplegic Association, there were no wonder drugs, and medical knowledge regarding spinal cord injuries was limited, to say the least. If you were paralyzed, your support system was likely made up of what you could organize for yourself. But not only did Stan survive, he thrived. He was, in the true sense, a pioneer. He searched for and reclaimed his life, he became happy and fulfilled, and he even made time to help others along the way.

I found other role models among disabled athletes; I could identify with them. In no time at all, Stan had me playing table tennis as well as other wheelchair sports. By late May I found myself in the Pacific Northwest Games for the Disabled table tennis singles finals, and a month later I was competing in the National Wheelchair Games in Montreal.

Meeting Stan Stronge changed my life, but his importance

to me as a role model was just beginning. I came to respect him immensely. Stan didn't offer any hollow keep-an-optimistic-outlook speeches. Instead, he challenged me with all of the great opportunities and rewards that were available to wheelchair-bound athletes through sports. Stan passed away a couple of years ago. He had been honoured by his country in 1981 with the Order of Canada, and recognized and respected by countless people, like me, that he helped and motivated. Stan always inspired me with his spirit and his upbeat, yet pragmatic attitude toward life. He inspired me with his selfless commitment to improve the lives of others. By being there for me, he helped me to realize the value of helping others.

When I came home from the Man In Motion World Tour I faced many decisions and so much uncertainty. I was going to need positive role models like Stan Stronge as never before. Amanda and I had been married soon after we returned and I quickly came to respect and admire Patrick Reid, her father. He was then just completing his duties as Commissioner-General for EXPO 86 and was about to embark on his posting as Canadian Consul in San Francisco. Patrick, I believe, lives his life with authority and dignity, and he has always been there for me when I've needed a little perspective. I have developed a real appreciation for his ability to reduce even the most confusing situation to its most basic elements, then devise an effective strategy for resolving it. He seems to be able to work easily with opposing sides, no matter how far apart, and still find a solution acceptable to both without violating anyone's fundamental principles. What I admire most about him is his integrity. He 'walks his talk', and always seems well aware of the boundaries that separate principle from convenience and expediency.

If I was to be as effective in my new world as Patrick Reid was in his, I knew I would have to develop the kinds of traits and skills he uses so constructively.

•

Identify three people who have had a significant impact on your life. Think about exactly what had an impact on you and why. Think about three people who have had a negative impact on you and why.

Now, try to identify ways in which you might emulate the positive and avoid the example of the negative role models in your own life.

Strategy: Identifying Re-Orienting Moments

Another way to sharpen awareness is to become alert to what we call re-orienting moments. These are moments that occur in everyone's life when you are suddenly struck with a particularly compelling thought or feeling. These moments can take the form of a new awareness, a realization or an insight. An every-day example of a re-orienting moment is the "aha" experience—that moment when something suddenly becomes clear. Something that has previously eluded you is now revealed; it's like being given the answer to a puzzle. Once enlightened, you can never go back to your previous state of unawareness.

The concept of the re-orienting moment is easy to understand. What is more difficult, however, is to listen and be receptive to these moments. When we are open to their influence, they can re-orient us. Often, they can help us to discover a meaningful re-direction. They can sometimes lead to an evaluation of one's self and what matters, often setting the stage for a major decision.

•

I remember an important moment in a conversation I had with another role model, Bob Proctor, who makes his living as an educator and human development trainer. We were talking about my current career situation and I was complaining about how stretched I felt. After the tour, I had continued my work trying to help people with disabilities achieve their potential. At the same time, I told him that I was interested in continuing to talk about the idea of personal motivation in my role as a keynote speaker. I told him how interested I was in moving more into this field, but that I felt swamped by all my other commitments. And besides, I really didn't know if I could make a go of it anyway.

He listened patiently, then furrowed his brow and looked straight into my eyes. "Rick, you just don't see it, do you? I'm watching you struggle trying to decide what to do with this gold mine of an opportunity you're sitting on. Take some time to know the area, to see the possibilities. Then, your commitment will come and the decision will be easy."

Bob was pointing out that my perspective was far too narrow. He said that I was too focused on keynote speaking, and not the bigger picture—the whole field of motivation. There were virtually endless possibilities, he said. I just needed to broaden my perspective. Bob wanted me to see that I was trying to over-analyze everything in an attempt to have it all wrapped in a nice, neat package before I started.

It was true; I'd allowed myself to be intimidated by my own lack of clarity and vision. Where was the guy who began an around-the-world tour with little more than a commitment and a few friends crazy enough to think that he could pull it off? Bob was simply holding up a mirror before me. He was telling me to reflect on the same principles that I had used throughout the Man In Motion World Tour. In a sense, he was chiding me for apparently not having learned anything from my own experience. It quickly became clear that I needed to go through the cycle again, applying the same principles and processes I had used on the tour in this situation and in the future. The lessons were indeed timeless and relevant. Essentially, he was saying, "Rick, you've selected your goal; shore up your vision, don't overplan, and get started!"

•

Have you ever experienced a re-orienting moment? Write down a description of what happened, and who else was involved, if anyone. In what ways did it affect your life? Did it lead to an important change or decision?

●

A final note on sharpening awareness. We want you to begin to build an awareness of yourself, enough to set a worthy personal change goal. But, don't get bogged down in trying to become fully aware. Awareness is a life-long undertaking and does not begin and end here. As you work your way through each step of the process, your awareness will deepen and expand as you discover new aspects of yourself. Self-discovery becomes an integral part of the change process.

STEP #1

SETTING YOUR GOAL

*I watched how people responded to Terry Fox,
and later, after his death, how they continued to
honour his spirit. They acknowledged
how much good came to so many from one
young man's dream.*

I didn't just wake up one day and decide that I was going to wheel around the world. The Man In Motion project began as an itch in the back of my mind in the days after I left the G. F. Strong Rehabilitation Centre and headed back to my Williams Lake home. At that time, it had nothing to do with disability awareness or fund raising; it had almost everything to do with pure physical challenge.

It was one of those kid's dreams where you lie on the grass staring up at the moon and imagining that you'll go there some day. Then, later, as I began to focus on marathoning and enjoyed some success, I realized that I really was physically and emotionally strong enough to wheel around the world—if I wanted to. But so what?

Sure, I could do it with my friends, a tent and a trailer. We could set our own pace—but was it worth it to take three years out of my life? I was working on my college degree in physical education and competing internationally in wheelchair sports. I didn't want to leave all that just so I could come home and say, "Well, I wheeled around the world." Big deal.

Then, in 1980, Terry Fox came striding along on a prosthetic leg, with his Marathon of Hope. He was going to run across Canada on sheer guts and determination to raise money for cancer research. It was his way of fighting back against the disease that cost him his leg. Terry and I had come to know one another—had become teammates and friends—through wheelchair basketball. I watched people respond to him, and later, after his death, how they continued to honour his spirit. They acknowledged how much good came to so many from one young man's dream. Somewhere along in there I realized *there was something missing from my own dream.*

By that time, I'd talked to scores of disabled people in my travels, and I had discovered what we had in common. No, not the disability factor. So what? That was obvious. What we had in common was that we all faced the same physical, emotional and mental barriers. We lived in a world that saw us, yet didn't know us. Sometimes we felt invisible; sometimes we were invisible. What I began to see was the impact that Terry had on raising awareness—in individuals, in communities, in governments. He made people see, see the invisible.

I enjoyed giving. It made me feel good to help others. So how about continuing Terry's theme? What if I made it the major focus of my wheelchair journey around the world? I could be the catalyst, the messenger, and in that role, perhaps I could help people with disabilities everywhere. It felt good, but the potential impact was staggering. And as an after-thought—and that's all it was—maybe I could raise not only awareness, but money as well. Money that would help people disabled by spinal cord injuries through research, rehabilitation, wheelchair sports and recreation programs.

At that moment, the moon-gazing 'what-ifs' ceased; the tour was no longer something I could do, it became something I had to do. The physical challenge had always been there, I had my mountain to climb. Only now I had a better reason for climbing it.

•

Now that you have begun to sharpen your awareness about what you would like to change, you must take the first step. You need to identify and commit to a definite goal. What is a goal? A goal is an end toward which a specific effort is directed. Goals can be large or small, simple or complicated. Regardless of their dimensions, goals are a vital force in life. They allow us to exert some control over our lives, and they give our lives meaning. By setting goals, we are making change happen. If we don't set goals, things just happen to us. In these changing times, goals provide stability by giving us direction and focus that is anchored within ourselves and not dependent upon others or events in our environment. Goals enable us to monitor our growth and development, and, most importantly, to shape the course of our lives.

Principle #1

Make your goals personally meaningful.

The goal you set, however big or small, must be worthwhile. To be worthwhile a goal needs to be anchored in personal meaning. A goal has personal meaning if it matters to you, if it has personal significance. What is meaningful to one person is not necessarily meaningful to another. 'Meaning' is an individually defined, subjective experience. What makes an activity meaningful has little to do with the objective value of an activity, but rather with what it represents or means to the person doing it. Therefore, to engage in meaningful goal-setting you must become your own authority about what is meaningful to you and actively resist the undue influence of others.

To be meaningful, a goal should be based on authentic personal motives. Your personal motives are the reasons behind what you do; they give meaning to your actions. Uncovering and establishing authentic motives enables you to set meaningful goals. Authentic motives exist when a person's thoughts, feelings, and actions are in harmony with one another. When you are inauthentic, you are 'out of tune' with yourself and unable to be genuine. You can engage in self-directed change, and you can decide, plan and take action to get things done and do this very effectively. But, if the goals you set are not based on authentic motives, then achieving them will be meaningless.

To have personal meaning, a goal should also be self-initiated. That is, the goal needs to be motivated from within you rather than imposed from the outside, or directed by other people or by your circumstances. For example, you can set a goal and achieve it, but if the motivation behind the goal is to please others or to gain their approval, achieving it will be meaningless. A good example of this dynamic would be the son or daughter who sets a career goal based upon parental desires, not his or her own aspirations.

The importance of meaningful goal-setting is that you are more likely to commit to goals that mean something to you. Making and keeping commitments results in a greater sense of success. Meaningful goal-setting facilitates a deeper involvement with and a more active participation in the world.

Wheeling around the world was indeed a physical challenge for Rick and, therefore, a worthwhile goal, but devoting three years to a purely physical challenge was not enough. What would succeeding mean? It was only after Terry Fox and his Marathon of Hope came along that some personal meaning emerged. When this meaning crystallized—to raise awareness of the potential of people with disabilities—a worthy goal was uncovered.

Strategy: Uncovering Personal Meaning

In your journal, jot down three things that are personally meaningful or significant to you, whether they are personal, interpersonal or career oriented.

For example, for Rick, when he was about to embark on the tour, three meaningful things were:

• Being a pioneer and pursuing unconventional, innovative goals.
• Being an athlete and undertaking physical challenges.
• Helping others.

Then, write down three things that are not meaningful. Sometimes to clarify what does matter, we have to first clarify what does not.

Some things which were not meaningful for Rick were:
• Maintaining the status quo by doing what is considered routine.
• Living a sedentary life.
• Being isolated and alone.

Finally, rank the three things that are meaningful to you in order of their importance.

Rick's priority was:
1. Helping others.
2. Being a pioneer and pursuing unconventional, innovative goals.
3. Being an athlete and undertaking physical challenges.

Principle #2

Make your goals personally challenging.

The goal you set must be challenging. At the same time, it should be realistic and attainable, not impossible to reach. It should be challenging enough to make you stretch, but not so far that you break. If the goal is unrealistic or too difficult, you will likely fail. On the other hand, if the goal is too easy, achieving it will seem insignificant and irrelevant. Therefore, the key is to find a balance between a goal that is challenging and your ability to meet that challenge.

Wheeling around the world may seem to be an unrealistic goal for some. Given Rick's five years of training it was challenging, but not unrealistic. Having achieved the title of best wheelchair marathoner in the world, this journey would be the ultimate marathon—one long wheelchair race broken into a series of marathons all strung together. Certainly, there was the physical challenge, but the greater challenge was to successfully communicate the message, the meaning behind the goal.

The concept of personal best is crucial here. Personal best means trying to be the best that you can be, given your unique personal circumstances, skills and abilities. Understanding your personal best requires a realistic self-appraisal. You must be able to identify your strengths and weaknesses as well as your limits and potential. It also involves defining your personal standards for success and failure. Many people do not reach their goals because they misguidedly seek perfection or someone else's standard of success. Setting unrealistic standards often renders the goal unattainable— so overwhelming that it keeps you from starting in the first place. Striving to achieve your personal best is always realistic and possible. As your goals are reached, new and higher goals can then be identified and sought after as your personal standards continue to be revised and upgraded.

•

Disabled athletes were first included in the Olympic Games in 1984, and the 1,500-metre wheelchair race had been chosen as an exhibition event. The Olympic qualifying races were to be held in New York the preceding June, and the eight highest finishers would go to Los Angeles and become a part of Olympic history.

While in training that April, I was testing a new wheelchair which had been giving us steering problems. Coming down a steep hill, I thought I had it under control, but I was going about 30 miles an hour when I hit a section of bumpy road surface. I went airborne and the chair flipped sideways. The result was a dislocated left shoulder and considerable road rash. I was taken to the hospital, where my arm was relocated. The prognosis was grim: I couldn't compete again until fall. There went my chance for the Olympics.

While I did listen to the doctor's medical advice, I also

knew I needed to define and set my own limits, to push myself to my potential. So, instead of focusing on my disappointment and the very real possibility that I would miss the opportunity of a lifetime, I threw myself into my rehab. I worked daily with my coach, Tim, on overall physical conditioning and specifically on my shoulder with my physiotherapist, Amanda. After only four weeks of treatment and reconditioning, I wheeled back onto the track and returned slowly to form. By the end of May, my 400-metre interval times were within .001 second of my pre-injury times. It looked like I would be going to New York for the qualifying races after all.

In New York there were three heats, and each time I was able to advance. The two semi-final heats remained, and from them only the eight fastest qualifiers would make it to the Games. I was in the first heat. I pushed as hard as I could, and placed fourth. Then I had to sit back helplessly and watch the second heat. It was so close I couldn't tell where I had placed. We had to wait until they announced the names. I knew who the first four would be based on their heat finishes. Fifth place was announced, then sixth; seventh place was called and still no Hansen. Finally, my name—the eighth-place finisher— came over the loudspeaker. I had managed to qualify by .001 second over the ninth-place competitor from Sweden.

I had placed eighth and barely qualified by the skin of my teeth. I've won world championships and gold medals, yet no other athletic success has ever matched the feeling of personal victory and fulfilment I carried away from New York. The accomplishment of doing my personal best and qualifying despite the challenge I faced made it my biggest success ever.

•

Strategy: Realistically Assessing Your Strengths and Weaknesses

In order to be able to set your goal and achieve an appropriate balance between challenge and possibility, it is important to develop a clear idea of your personal abilities and limitations.

Try not to put a value judgement on each listing. Instead, try to be realistic and accurate in your evaluation of yourself. In your journal, write down your strengths. Next, write down your weaknesses. Now, honestly assess both. See if any of the weaknesses are 'fatal'. Can your strengths outweigh your shortcomings?

Here are Rick's strengths and weaknesses in relation to the tour:

Strengths	Weaknesses
Athletic	Stubborn
Mentally tough	Perfectionistic
Caring	Idealistic
Risk-taker	Not well organized
Honest	No specific project experience
Team builder/player	
Communicator	

Principle #3

Make your goals specific and definable.

Keep the goal challenging, but break it down into small, manageable parts. Be specific and concrete, and clearly define your goal. For example, a general goal of physical fitness needs to be translated into something more specific such as starting a physical fitness program, including learning about nutrition, relaxation techniques and exercise. Or, the general goal of increasing your income needs to be translated into something such as consulting a financial advisor for advice on how to increase your investment income and buy a home. Improving your leadership skills as a general goal may need to be defined in terms of reading four books on leadership skills and enrolling in a leadership seminar or training program.

Making your goal specific and definable is important because it allows you to measure, monitor and evaluate your progress. If a goal has been adequately specified and defined, you are then in a position to know exactly when you have completed it. The goal of the Man In Motion World Tour was to raise awareness of the potential of people with disabilities. Measuring awareness was not realistic so the goal was translated into objective terms—raising $10 million for spinal cord injury research and rehabilitation.

Strategy: Identifying Your Goal

Refer to your notes from the Preparing for Change section where you identified aspects of yourself that you wanted to improve, develop or change. Here, you will need to translate those responses into specific goals. Given the number of areas from which to choose and the multitude of possibilities, remember to select a goal that is right for you at this particular moment in your life. Goals can be set in a variety of different areas.

Here are some examples:

Types of Personal Goals
- Overcoming a fear, such as public speaking
- Stopping a self-destructive pattern, such as smoking
- Getting physically fit
- Exploring and developing your spiritual self

Types of Interpersonal Goals
- Improving communication skills
- Volunteering your time
- Increasing intimacy with others
- Making new friends

Types of Career Goals
- Seeking a promotion
- Changing careers
- Improving leadership skills
- Increasing income

For example, here were Rick's goals in 1984:

- Be a physical education teacher
- Train for a fourth wheelchair marathon World Championship
- Wheel around the world in wheelchair to help others
- Learn how to fly
- Get married
- Become financially independent

In order to make them more specific and definable, he revised them to read:

- Take two years of teacher training to qualify myself to teach physical education in the provincial school system
- Train to win a fourth wheelchair marathon World Championship by July 1985
- Wheel 24,901.55 miles around the world in eighteen months to raise public awareness about capabilities of people with disabilities
- Enroll in pilot training, obtain pilot's licence and fly solo
- Get married and start a family
- Through investments in the stock market make $1 million

Now make your own list of possible goals. Remember to:

- List meaningful goals. Ask yourself the following questions as a guide: Does this goal matter to me? Why and how does it matter? What is the reason or motive for my goal? Who would I be doing it for?
- List challenging but realistic goals. Ask yourself the following questions as a guide: Is this goal challenging enough for me? Is this goal attainable? Do I know what my personal best will be?
- List specific and definable goals. Ask yourself the following questions as a guide: Is this goal specific? Have I defined my goal clearly? How will I measure my progress? How will I know when I have reached my goal?

Next, rank each of your goals in light of what matters to you, as you identified it in the Preparing for Change section.

This was Rick's ranking:

1. Wheel 24,901.55 miles around the world in eighteen months to raise public awareness about capabilities of people with disabilities

2. Train to win a fourth wheelchair marathon World Championship by July 1985

3. Take two years of teacher training to qualify myself to teach physical education in the provincial school system

4. Get married and start a family

5. Through investments in the stock market make $1 million

6. Enroll in pilot training, obtain pilot's licence and fly solo

Now it's time to select your goal. Usually, it is best to pursue one personal change goal at a time. However, there are people who effectively manage several simultaneously. If you think you can handle it, go right ahead. For those of you who are less confident, we recommend that you try a single goal first, then as you familiarize yourself with this process you can add goals that reflect your comfort level. Also, the goal you choose may not necessarily be the most important one on the list, but it may be the goal that fits best with your current situation.

Principle #4

Commit to your goal.

Once you have selected your goal, you must commit to it. To commit is to become deeply involved with your goal. You cannot be deeply involved with or committed to something that lacks meaning. Therefore, your choice of a worthwhile goal is crucial. Ultimately, committing to your goal means committing to yourself, and taking yourself seriously.

The purpose of making a commitment is to give yourself 'staying power', the power you must have in order to keep going in the face of obstacles. The stronger your commitment, the stronger the chances of success.

Strategy: Making Your Commitment

One practical way to strengthen your commitment is to make your goal public. Going public can add incentive by increasing personal accountability. You can do this in many ways. Make a public declaration about your goal to a friend, announce your intentions at a club meeting or join someone in the pursuit of a common goal.

The most important commitment, however, is the one you make to yourself. To assist you in making your personal commitment the following commitment contract is a way of externalizing your intentions and making them explicit. Many people find that the ritual of signing this contract is valuable and helps during trying times when motivation lags.

COMMITMENT CONTRACT

I, _____ , have set a personal change goal to:

_____

_____

By signing this agreement, I am committing myself to the completion of my goal.

Signature:

_____

Witness:

_____

By signing this agreement, you are taking the first step. You have identified your goal and committed to it. As you move through the other steps in the change process, your commitment will inevitably deepen and broaden. By the end of the process, your commitment will not merely be something you did, it will be a personal quality you have developed— that is, the ability to commit to yourself and to your goals. Through pursuing self-directed change, you are committing yourself to shaping the course of your own life.

Ultimately, making a commitment is essential to successfully achieving your goal. However, your commitment does not have to be total or complete at this exact point. You may find that, in going through the next two steps, envisioning and planning for your goal, you are able to more fully realize and solidify your commitment.

•

The final piece to the puzzle was still missing. If we were going to tour the world, we must not only open doors, but borders as well. An effort such as ours would need the sponsorship of an organization that was recognized and accepted throughout the world, an organization whose status alone would help get us a hearing from the governments of other countries. Without this kind of assistance, it would be next to impossible to enter and exit other countries with any ease. We would need to arrange visas, and organize the routing through each country and gain the support of the disability organizations along the way. And, of course, we'd need to do the hundreds of other things that had to be done if this was to be anything more than just a push around the world in a chair with wheels.

But for a chance meeting with Bill McIntosh, a friend I'd met through marathon racing, we might never have found the missing piece. He suggested that I use EXPO 86, the world exposition to be held in Vancouver, as a vehicle to achieve that objective. The theme of EXPO was Man In Motion— transportation and communication. It seemed to fit. Bingo! The last piece to the puzzle.

This, then, was a turning point. I stopped dreaming and,

for the first time, actually committed myself to the project. Prior to that moment, I had no actual responsibility or concern about success or failure. Sure, I had committed myself to the tour, but I was only accountable to myself. Once I confided in my close friends and family, I had upped the ante considerably. By doing that, others now expected me not only to get started but to finish. To just walk away now would be difficult, to say the least. I would lose credibility if I couldn't get it started; I would be embarrassed and ashamed if I started and couldn't finish. I suppose, even then, I still could have walked away from it with minimal damage. I'm sure those close to me would have understood.

However, when I broadened my commitment to include promises to other individuals and organizations, the obligations and responsibilities increased accordingly. When I first approached EXPO officials asking for sponsorship, I remember thinking, what if they say "yes"? Then the whole world will be watching; I'll not only be doing the tour, I will be promoting EXPO, Vancouver and my country. With each successive patron's pledge, my fear increased, but so did my commitment. The strength of my commitment came from inside. The external incentives and pressures were still there, but this tour had become significant; it had become a part of me.

Summary

Step #1

Setting Your Goal

Principles

#1. Make your goals personally meaningful.
#2. Make your goals personally challenging.
#3. Make your goals specific and definable.
#4. Commit to your goal.

STEP #2

CULTIVATING YOUR PERSONAL VISION

Forrest Andersen

*I visualized the moment I would start wheeling
on the Great Wall of China. It was as if
the Great Wall was a metaphor for the entire trip
around the world . . . it contained all the obstacles
and triumphs.*

*B*ack in 1984, when Tim Frick and I were planning the Man In Motion project in the basement of my apartment building, something really significant happened as we pored over atlases. As we focused on Asia, I was almost instantly bombarded by vivid images and thoughts of wheeling my chair along the Great Wall of China.

In my mind, I could see the Great Wall off in the distance stretched from horizon to horizon, a huge imposing structure set against the rugged terrain. I could picture myself in my wheelchair—dwarfed by the size of the wall—passing through deep green valleys and struggling up the steepest slope to reach the highest point. Since the plan was to be there in late March, it would be relatively cool. But, I could see the sweat build on my body as my pace slowed with the steepness of the slope. I started to think about what an amazing feat it was to build the wall and to have it still standing after so many years. I also thought about what an amazing feat it was going to be to complete the tour.

It was as if the Great Wall was the metaphor for the entire trip around the world; it contained all the obstacles and triumphs. The vision seemed to embody what lay ahead. There was such a contrast between then and now. The wall was built at a time when disability meant certain death. And here I was, with a significant disability, planning to wheel across it thousands of years later. This thought became to me an instant symbol of what could be accomplished over time and with persistence. It was a personal symbol that there are no walls in life too big to climb. After that vision, I decided that the only thing I wanted personally from the tour was a picture of *me wheeling the Great Wall. I would hang it on my bedroom wall as a reminder of those symbols for the rest of my life.*

•

You have completed the first step of the process by identifying a definite goal. The next step involves envisioning your goal. Webster's defines vision as "the act or power of imagination." Through cultivating a personal vision, you bring your goal to life.

Visualization is part of learning how to focus your mental energy. By using your creative mind you can better bring about desired and valued results. Combined with awareness, your imagination empowers you to creatively shape your future.

For years, the power of visualization has been used by a variety of people in a variety of ways, such as athletes to improve performance, entertainers to reduce anxiety, executives to reduce stress, those afflicted with illness to improve health, and many others to achieve success.

The personal vision you must cultivate is a mental expression of what it would be like for you to realize your goal. Using the power of your imagination to create a clear, strong vision makes your goal more specific and increases the possibility of reaching it. It is harder to strive toward a goal on the horizon if you cannot see it.

Whether your goal is as grand as a world tour or more conventional such as a career change, it helps to begin with a clear vision.

Principle #1

Create your vision.

The other thing I envisioned was the last day. I would be coming home to Vancouver after more than two years on the road. What a feeling that was; to picture Vancouver just off in the distance from my Hastings Street vantage point. Vancouver, a bright jewel, nestled between the mountains and the ocean. I knew it would be a clear, sunny day. I could feel the heat rising off the pavement. The crowd would be cheering; there would be thousands of people coming out to rejoice in the spirit of what the tour was all about. Somehow, I knew that it would happen just that way.

•

You experience the world by gathering information through your senses. The following strategy is designed to help you deepen and enrich your ability to visualize your goal by using as many of your senses as possible. Visualization is a powerful, straightforward technique that is easy to learn but requires practice. Don't expect instant results.

Strategy: Using Guided Visualization

One way to help bring clarity to your vision is through guided visualization. Through this process, you can relax and go inside yourself to find the images and sensations which make up your vision. It begins with relaxation. You may find it easier to work through this process by having a friend read the following text to you or by making a tape recording to play back as you relax.

Take a few moments to settle down comfortably. Close your eyes and become aware of your body. Turn your attention away from outside events and notice what is going on inside you. Notice any discomfort, and see if you can find a more comfortable position. Notice what parts of your body emerge into your awareness, and which parts of your body seem vague and indistinct. If you become aware of a tense area within your body, see if you can release that tension. If not, deliberately tense that part, to see what muscles you are tensing, and then relax once more.

Now focus your attention on your breathing. Become aware of all the details of your breathing. Feel the air move in through your nose or mouth, feel it move down your throat and feel your chest and belly move as you breathe. Now, imagine your breathing as gentle waves along the shore, and that each wave slowly washes some tension from your body, and releases you even more . . .

Now, in this relaxed and calm state, 'see' yourself attaining your goal. Make every effort to imagine this scene as vividly as possible.

Rather than merely watch what is happening, use all your senses to experience the scene. Take your time and fill the canvas as richly as possible. As an aid, ask yourself the following questions:

Sight:
What images do I see around me? What details do I see of myself, of others?
Example: I could picture myself wheeling toward Vancouver, seeing it off on the horizon, and I could see thousands of people lining the streets, coming out to welcome me home.

Sound:
What sounds do I hear around me, from others or myself?
Example: I could hear the cheers of the crowd on that last day.

Touch:
Are there any physical sensations? Where are they coming from?
Example: I could feel the heat rising off the pavement. I could feel my heart pounding.

Taste:

Are their any distinctive tastes in your vision?

Example: The sweat ran down my face, leaving a salty taste.

Smell:

Are their any distinctive scents, smells, odours?

Example: I could smell the sea breeze coming off Burrard Inlet.

Awareness:

What am I aware of?

Example: I imagined that the tour would make a difference in the lives of others and change my whole life forever

Strategy: Recording Your Vision

In your journal, describe your vision using all your sensory sources of information: sight, sound, touch, taste, smell and awareness.

Having broken down your vision into its respective parts, now it's time to put it back together. Write out your personal vision in its entirety. Stay in the first person, using 'I' statements and action statements whenever possible. Be as imaginative as you can and try not to censor yourself. Let yourself get carried away by your own imagination.

Example: I imagine myself returning to beautiful Vancouver after wheeling around the world. Thousands of people line the streets; I hear them cheering me on, rejoicing in the spirit of the tour. I imagine that it will be a clear sunny day and I will be able to feel the heat coming off the concrete as I wheel into Oakridge Mall. I will be able to smell the sea breeze, and it will be a glorious day when my vision and reality merge. I imagine that my efforts will not have been in vain, that we will have been able to make a difference in the lives of others, that we will have created a greater awareness of the potential of people with disabilities, and that we will have challenged people to remove those barriers that stand in the way.

You might find it helpful to carry your vision around with you. You can review it and refresh your memory whenever you need a shot of inspiration or motivation. Keep this vision in the forefront of your mind. We will ask you to refer to it in later steps.

•

Now, you have actively explored achieving your goal. Is the goal still meaningful to you? Are you still committed to your goal? If the answer to either of these questions is "no," you may need to go back to Step #1 to review your personal motives. You may need to select a goal that better fits the basic criteria, one that is personally meaningful and challenging, and one to which you are ready and willing to commit.

If you have difficulty with this step, don't be overly concerned. Some people work better with their imaginations than others. What do you do if your vision is unclear, despite your efforts? In this case, go on to the next step, which we call planning. Sometimes, if the vision is difficult to picture or is vague, the detailed examination which is fundamental to planning helps to strengthen and crystallize it.

Summary

Step #2

Cultivating Your Personal Vision

Principle

#1. Create your vision.

STEP #3

PLANNING TO REACH YOUR GOAL

The tour was a major logistical task.
It was a team effort of which I was simply the
symbolic focal point.

Two years of planning went into the Man In Motion World Tour before we set off. In the beginning, there was only me, my dream, and a handful of friends and family members who believed in me.

The plan went something like this. EXPO 86 offered an ideal opportunity to ensure a credible and reputable sponsor for the project. I negotiated with them to carry their 'Man In Motion' message around the globe. They agreed to sanction the tour, thus ensuring some media coverage. They also allowed us to incorporate their slogan into our name. Most importantly, they agreed in principle to provide us with a portion of their $1 million budget for the development of off-site activities.

I then approached the British Columbia Paraplegic Foundation with this plan. They agreed to sponsor us, and the Man In Motion World Tour became a separate project with its own board of directors. They also managed to come up with $10,000 seed money. The next logical step was setting up home base, a central office from which to manage the tour. The office staff would be responsible for fund raising, media relations and ensuring that those of us on the road crew had all the operational necessities.

Then, EXPO 86 dropped the bomb. Faced with a soaring budget, they cancelled the program which contained our funding. Reality set in with a vengeance. There we were, left high and dry. Until the devastating news from EXPO 86, I was feeling pretty good about the way things had fallen into place. I was half right: things hadn't fallen into place, things were just falling.

What the heck! We'd come too far to stop now. I had decided to put three years of my life into giving this my best shot. If it didn't work out, at least I'd know I had tried.

•

Now that your objective is clear, the next step is to translate your goal and your vision into action. To do this you need a plan. In planning, you are really accepting responsibility for what is to happen and taking charge of getting things done.

Plans serve several important functions. They provide a framework and a structure to guide you toward your objective. A plan helps keep you on track and enables you to be more efficient, thereby maximizing your chances of success. Plans also provide the means by which you can monitor progress toward your goal. Perhaps most importantly, detailing your intentions on paper is one more step toward deepening your commitment to your goal.

Your plan will be unique—singular to you as well as customized to fit your goal. Naturally, the more complex the goal, the more complex the plan will need to be. Planning, in and of itself, does not get you to the finish line, but *good* planning helps. Some people will be better at planning than others. If planning is not your strong suit, don't be overly concerned. Read the chapter, and do the best you can. Plans have a way of clarifying themselves as you go.

Principle #1

Establish a guiding philosophy.

For your plan, you need to develop a set of philosophical principles consistent with what is personally meaningful to you and designed with your specific goal in mind. These principles will form a foundation that will guide and direct you as you implement your plan. They will act as a compass to help you stay on course. They will also serve as a reminder of that which is important to you and will help you make difficult decisions that may arise as you put your plan into action.

Example: Rick's Philosophical Principles for the Man In Motion World Tour
- Maintain a total commitment to my objective. Other things such as relationships or being a tourist must always take second place.
- Maintain my physical health.
- Maintain my integrity.
- Be honest.
- Learn from my mistakes. Work at continuous improvement.

•

One of my guiding principles for the tour was to be honest. The goal was to wheel 24,901.55 miles—the circumference of the earth. Each mile would be painstakingly recorded to ensure accuracy. I would measure my distance travelled each day as accurately as possible to within a hundredth of a mile. I was determined never to draft along behind another wheeler or the motorhome in order to reduce my wind resistance.

One day in California, I was enticed to compromise this principle. We were en route to Sacramento, the state capital, for a function. We were late and I was wheeling against some pretty incredible headwinds—25 to 30 miles per hour along the river. My speed had decreased from 9 mph to 6 mph, so I decided that during one 27-mile segment I would wheel behind the motorhome in order to make it to the event on time. We made the event, but by the end of that day I felt terrible about compromising my principles—so much so that I asked that nine miles be taken off my daily total to compensate for the advantage I had gained.

There were many times throughout the remainder of the tour that I was tempted to draft because of injury, fatigue or frustration, but I always remembered the lesson and the principle. In fact, I ended up wheeling an extra 250 miles as 'insurance'. I wanted my record to be indisputable even under the toughest scrutiny.

•

Strategy: Recording Your Guiding Principles

In your journal, write down your set of guiding philosophical principles. They'll be there in black and white to remind you what you believe in, any time you feel tempted to stray from the course you have set yourself.

Principle #2

Be realistic.

In order to create a quality plan, you need to realistically assess your strengths and weaknesses in light of your goal. You may need to refer to your notes on strengths and weaknesses from Step #1. In this way, you can plan to utilize your strengths in the greatest possible way and, as well, you can plan in advance to compensate for your shortcomings. Accurately assessing where you might need help will enable you to build in the necessary supports in advance, and in so doing, you will be maximizing your chances of success.

Being realistic also involves the ability to recognize and anticipate potential conflicts, either at-large or interpersonally, that might help or hinder you as you strive to reach your goal. You need to minimize or eliminate things that may interfere with moving toward your goal, while maximizing others that enhance movement toward it.

For example, if your goal is to improve your grades, then a key component is studying. If you normally have a radio on, but recognize that music interferes with your concentration, then you would turn that radio off to minimize intrusive sound and maximize quiet in a focused effort to meet your goal.

Another example may involve anticipating the reaction of other people. If you need to return to school in order to reach your goal, you may need to anticipate the reaction of family members and the impact of your decision on them. They might not always be delighted with your decision, if your goal conflicts with their own. After accurately anticipating their reactions and in consideration of their feelings, you may decide to return to school part-time in order to accommodate your children or spouse. When potential conflicts in your environment are minimized your chances for success are maximized.

To achieve the goal of wheeling around the world, some things in Rick's life were necessarily minimized while others were maximized. For example, the timing of the tour coincided with another of Rick's goals, which was pursuing a university degree. To manage these competing goals, time conflicts were anticipated. The tour was the clear priority. Therefore, one goal, education, had to be compromised in order to meet the needs of the other, the tour. Committing to the tour meant that the last two years of university would be spread over a four-year period. Coursework was fit in around competitions and training for the ultimate marathon. Then, it was put on hold altogether. Rick began his last university project just before leaving on the Man In Motion World Tour, and he graduated en route in April 1987, a month before he returned home.

Strategy: Dividing Your Goal into Key Components and Tasks

One way of realistically assessing what lies ahead of you is dividing up your goal into its key components and tasks. Tasks are all the little things that need to get done. Components are major groupings of tasks. Organizing what needs to be done in this fashion helps to bring order to what might at first seem like a haystack of things to do. And, it helps you to assign priority, to do what's most important first.

Key Components

Here's where you identify and list all the key components necessary to achieve your goal. What are the main categories of things you need to do to reach your objective?

Example: Here are some of the key components for the Man In Motion World Tour

Key Component 1. Planning for road crew.

Key Component 2. Establishing route.

Key Component 3. Raising funds for operations.

Key Component 4. Setting up home base.

Key Component 5. Raising money for Legacy Trust Fund.

Key Component 6. Recruiting volunteers.

Key Component 7. Publicizing tour.

Key Component 8. Preparing physically to wheel.

Key Component 9. Obtaining support from service groups.

List your key components.

Tasks

Next, identify and list the tasks that need to be accomplished for each of the key components you have listed. Keep your tasks realistic and attainable. Tasks which are unreasonably hard are seldom achieved, and those too easy usually produce results of little value. As much as possible, break your tasks into small, manageable parts. Also, strive to be specific and concrete. Keeping tasks small and specific enables you to monitor your progress and will help signal completion.

Example:
Key Component 1. Planning for road crew.
Tasks:

- Identify roles and responsibilities
- Select crew members
- Train crew members
- Obtain motorhome to transport crew
- Identify equipment and clothing requirements
- Recruit sponsor for uniforms and equipment
- Plan food requirements
- Establish medical support
- Obtain wheelchairs and equipment
- Complete trial run

•

When you're planning a trip around the world, it's kind of helpful, perhaps even essential, that you know your destination before you start. This is particularly true when the guy out front is in a wheelchair. Armed with British Columbia Automobile Association road maps and bicycle tour road atlases, my friend Tim and I went down to the basement of my apartment block and began laying out possible routes. It took us three weeks—one route per week.

The first one was 65,000 miles long. Great, if I wanted to be out there for seven years. I was committed, but there is a limit. We decided we had best try again. The second was 30,000 miles. Better, but still too long. The third was 24,000 including zigzags to compensate for oceans that tended to get in the way. Well, the circumference of the earth was 24,901.55 miles. That seemed an appropriate target. With that as our guide, we finalized a route based on political, geographic and climatic conditions that would allow us to visit as many countries as possible.

The question was, how much could I wheel each day of this journey? In order for me to determine that figure, I had to take a series of long-term tests of my threshold performance—what I could endure over sustained periods. Following a series of exercises which monitored my heart rate and conditioning, we determined that I would be able to wheel a total of 70 miles a day on a long-term basis, at a pace of approximately 9 mph. That determination made it much easier for us to plan our daily itinerary and allowed organizers to plan events around our progress.

Planning something as physically demanding as the Man In Motion World Tour, it was essential for me to be ready for the challenge. I had been training and competing in wheelchair sports for five years before starting around the world, but all my training had been based on 23-mile wheeling sessions. But, to keep yourself going in any sort of endurance event you have to establish goals-within-goals, carrots dangling out there in front of you to break the ordeal into mental and physical segments. Physically and psychologically that was what I'd programmed myself to do: three marathons per day with regular short breaks during each wheel, and two-hour rest periods between sessions.

•

One of the more challenging tasks was specifying the equipment and supplies that would be needed for five people for a period of two years. Here's what the list looked like at the start of the tour:

Tour essentials:
- *Wheelchair*
- *Spare wheelchair parts including tires, frame*
- *Eighty pairs of deerskin curling gloves*
- *Dress clothes*
- *Roofing tar*
- *Tools*
- *Kitchen appliances (e.g. blender)*

- *Fifteen bottles of Shur-grip*
- *Stick 'n' Sew*
- *Bicycles*
- *Communal socks and underwear*

There were good and logical reasons for every item. I'd used the curling gloves to wheel for a long time, and figured I'd average a pair a week. Handpushing 70 miles required 80 strokes per minute, 10 hours per day, which totalled 48,000 strokes per wheeling day. Eighty pairs seemed a good guess. The roofing tar was to spread on the gloves for a better grip on the pushrims.

Nike was supplying our tour clothing: twelve sets of clothing for me—I'd be in and out a lot and if the weather got bad, I'd have to change at each rest break—and four sets apiece for the others. We'd need dress gear for banquets, official meetings and such. Stick 'n' Sew to put the sponsorship patches on my clothes. Bicycles for the crew members who would be riding beside me. The blender for food preparation in the motorhome. And, of course, tools.

As I recall, the underwear didn't start out as communal property. At first, all the guys had their own. Then, as the tour pace got more frantic, they got mixed together on laundry runs and wound up in one big sack to be drawn upon as needed. That worked until I started getting careless with the roofing tar, at which point anything with tar on it was mine and the boys shared the rest. Eventually, I had tar over everything, and we were back to communal undies.

●

For each of the key components involved in reaching your goal, set out the tasks.

Strategy: Establishing Timelines

Another essential part of effective planning is establishing realistic timelines. First, you need to establish an overall timeline for reaching your goal. Then, you need to establish a realistic time frame for completion of each of the key components. You may also find it helpful to estimate timelines for completing individual tasks.

Example:

Goal: To wheel around the world in a wheelchair.
Estimated start date: Spring 1983
Estimated finish date: October 1986

Key Component 1. Planning for road crew.
Estimated start date: March 1984
Estimated finish date: March 1985

Task. Select crew members.
Estimated start date: March 1984
Estimated finish date: November 1984

Once you have worked out a detailed schedule, draw your timeline on a line graph like the one shown below. Draw a diagonal line from the bottom left corner of the graph to the upper right corner to indicate the overall time-frame for your goal. The line naturally moves upward as in the example because each component you complete moves you closer to your goal; the effect is naturally additive. Place dots at either end of the line. The dot at the left represents your start date. Write the actual start date beside it. The dot at the other end of the line signifies the estimated finish date. Now, mark an X on the line for each key component that needs to be completed. Number each component. Now, on the horizontal line draw a corresponding X for each component. From that X draw a line down and write the corresponding component on the line. As you start and complete a key component, mark your achievement on the timeline. In this way you will be able to track your progress toward your goal.

Example:

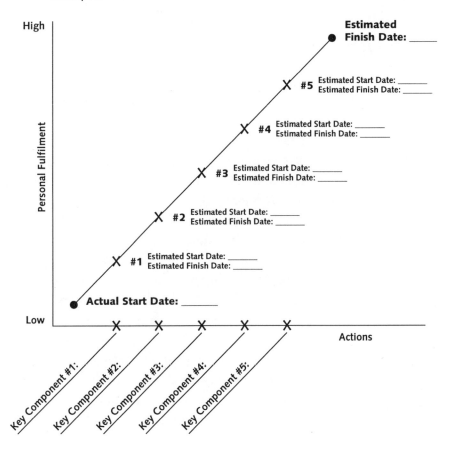

Principle #3

Recognize that there is strength in numbers.

No matter what your goal, you will likely need other people to help you accomplish it, at least to some degree, at some point. Even if you consider yourself a loner, chances are you will use a tool, take a course or follow a piece of advice, all of which involve benefitting from the experience of someone else. You're reading this book, aren't you?

In constructing your plan, it is important that you *actively* seek out and utilize the help of others. Don't try to do it all yourself and don't be afraid to ask for help. Help comes in many forms including support and encouragement, constructive feedback, direct resources and advice. Once you've asked for it, you need to be open to receiving the help of others. Support can come from individuals— friends, family members and counsellors—as well as from groups such as churches, clubs or professional organizations. The quarterback may receive the star billing, but without linemen to block for him and receivers to catch his passes, he'd spend the entire game running for his life, or flat on his back. We all are interdependent—it's human nature. So, take some comfort and gain strength from the knowledge that you are not alone.

One particularly useful type of individual help is a *mentor*. A mentor can be anyone who has successfully achieved goals similar to the ones that you want to accomplish, and who has agreed to provide advice and encouragement to you. Over the course of attaining your goal, your relationship with your mentor can help keep you pointed in the right direction, and provide you with a reliable source of encouragement when the going gets tough.

In addition to help from others, use the resources of libraries, newspapers, computer networks or television in the pursuit of your goal. Keep in mind, you don't have to re-invent the wheel. A wealth of information exists out there; you just have to zero in and gain access.

Strategy: Recruiting Your Team

Who will help you reach your goal? You need to be willing to ask for assistance or advice from those in a position to be helpful. Recruit your team informally from your own circle of friends and family, or from a formal group like business associates or club members. Your goal, of course, will determine the composition of the group.

•

A lot of people think that the Man In Motion World Tour succeeded because Rick Hansen—this intrepid soul—braved the elements and faced the world all by himself. That's the farthest thing from the truth. The reality of the tour? Eventually, there were thousands of people working together. The Man In Motion World Tour had a board of directors, forty people in the central office, regional and local coordinators across the country and around the world. We had thousands of volunteers. We had marketing people, corporations, fundraisers, salespeople and people in government helping us. It was a major logistical task, and it was a team effort of which I was simply the symbolic focal point.

•

Learn from the example of your role models, seek advice from your mentor or look to the experts for help. For example, if your goal is physical fitness, you may want to hire a trainer. Or, you may want to organize schedules with a spouse or friend to help motivate you. Select those who can offer their skill, advice, support or strength to help you realize your goal.

I brought in four stand-by's—people to finish the tour for me if I didn't or couldn't. With Terry Fox's experience in mind, I kept asking myself—how would I feel, what would I have done if I was injured and couldn't finish, or I got run over by a truck? I also didn't want to take so much ownership of the thing that it would fail if I couldn't wheel the distance. I saw myself as the vehicle, not the central force of the tour.

•

It is important to establish roles, obligations and expectations for each member of your team. Then, look at the plan you have developed and assign appropriate tasks to each of them. Remember that the members of your team may have complementary strengths where you have weaknesses and be willing to support you where you need them most.

•

In the beginning, I was doing everything. As the tour evolved, I started to delegate specific tasks to others. For instance, there was Tim Frick. He served as on-road tour manager. His job was to ensure that I was physically ready to wheel around the world and that the logistical requirements for the road crew were in place. He was selected for this role because he was my coach and had long been involved in my training schedule. He was also a teacher and had some administrative background. Don Alder, another friend, took the role of equipment manager. He was good with his hands and became quite knowledgeable in wheelchair mechanics; he filled this role admirably. Lee Gibson, my cousin, was a natural nurturer and was very concerned about my health, so he became the tour cook. He was also good at problem solving and became the person you would go to with special requests. The basics were in place, but as the planning requirements became more specific, we knew we would need more specialized levels of assistance.

Principle #4

Realize that no plan is perfect.

Although the ideal is to plan ahead as much as possible, reality presents the unexpected, conditions change, and so must your plan. In keeping with the notion of being realistic, you need to be prepared to adjust and modify your plan. Expect to improvise. Flexibility and adaptability, then, are the keys. Learn to consider being adaptable and flexible as skills, not just something you are forced to do because of circumstances. Be willing to bring out the giant eraser and change your plan, if you need to.

Remember, the whole purpose of the planning step is to get into position to act. If a goal is ever to be reached, there comes a point at which you must stop planning and take action. No plan is ever perfect. We plan enough to get going. A balance always needs to be found between overplanning and underplanning. Overplanning may lead to delays and missed opportunities; too little planning may lead to hasty or irresponsible action, or a false start. Either may ultimately lead to failure. No plan is ever complete nor even entirely clear before you must take the next step. But, through taking that step, plans that at first blush seem unclear do evolve and crystallize. The around-the-world tour was the goal, but the plan was far from complete before the tour began.

•

About two months before we were about to leave, we had to deal with a 'revolt' of some office staff members. For all sorts of reasons, they wanted to delay the start date. They argued that we needed more planning, more funding, more preparation and more staff. They wanted all the i's dotted and the t's crossed before we left. They gave me an ultimatum: delay until April 1 or preferably August 1, yet even then they wouldn't guarantee they'd be with us after April. They went on to say that if I did not comply the majority of them would quit.

I listened to each and every one of their concerns and then took some time away from the office to reflect. I sought out two of my friends and talked it over with them at length. I knew we would be delayed a little; I still wasn't totally recovered from a recent injury I'd had in training, and we didn't even have our motorhome. We weren't even close to raising enough money to cover the costs of the tour, and that meant that it was impossible to effectively plan the entire route before leaving. Truth be told, we only had enough money to last a couple of months. We had tapped out all our local options from people who were good-heartedly supporting a gutsy idea they thought would fail.

To me, the only way to secure additional financial support was to get out there, sell it to people that we could do it, that we could make the dream a reality. In fact, the longer we were delayed, the less chance we had of finishing during EXPO 86. We wanted to finish in the 1986 calendar year; a world's fair couldn't exactly be rescheduled to meet our timetable. Further delays of any significance also meant a greater chance that we would miss the good weather seasons en route—an element critical to the overall plan.

Finally, I returned to the rebels and said, "You're right. We can't leave on March 1st, so we'll have to delay to March 21st. We need three more weeks to get our motorhome. Any of you who want to quit, go for it. We appreciate all of your help." A number of them did quit. A couple of them came back once they knew I was serious.

After two years of planning, I simply felt there could be no more delays—we had to take the plunge and leave. There is a point when you must act on your plans; talk is cheap . . . and safe. Even if we had another two years of planning it wouldn't have been enough. Even the best possible plan could not predict weather or political conditions six months ahead and *thousands of miles away. If we waited until the perfect plan was in place, we'd never start; we would miss the window of opportunity and the dream would just fade away. It would become one of those ideas that never got off the ground, the kind you talk about with regrets amid small talk over drinks with friends. "If only. . . ." That was not the way I wanted this dream to end.*

Summary

Step #3

Planning to Reach Your Goal

Principles

#1. Establish a guiding philosophy.
#2. Be realistic.
#3. Recognize that there is strength in numbers.
#4. Realize that no plan is perfect.

STEP #4

TAKING RISKS

*When I started the tour, I was never sure that I
could do it, but I was sure that I could try.
Much of the time I simply felt overwhelmed by the
immensity of the task before me and the sheer
uncertainty of it all.*

March 21, 1985. A couple of hundred well-wishers gathered in the auditorium of a Vancouver shopping mall to help send us off. I remember sitting on the stage during the ceremonies, glancing over the faces in the crowd and seeing the occasional odd, doubting look. I was convinced that many of them really didn't believe that what we were about to do was possible—24,901.55 miles through 34 countries in 19 months. I was convinced that they had come not because we were likely to succeed, but because we had the courage to try.

I tried to listen to the various presentations, but my thoughts seemed to dart one after another in a dozen directions. I was vaguely aware of the speakers' words of praise and encouragement that drifted out over the crowd. I heard words of optimism from the mouths of others as well as my own, yet all the while I was wondering, "What the heck have I gotten myself into?"

There was no way we were ready; we were disorganized and poorly prepared. We had just about enough money to get us to Texas—about two months. For the last four months, I'd been recovering from a dislocated shoulder and still needed more rehab time. The weather was foul. If we'd started on schedule, March 1, we would have begun with good weather, a strong wind at our backs, strong enough to have blown us halfway to San Diego. But there had been delays, and now we would be getting underway in rotten, rainy weather with winds from the south ready to work on my face like sandpaper. Perhaps it was all an omen . . . the way it was going to be.

Logically, this was just not a good time to start. But, if we waited until everything was perfect, we could wait for a month . . . or a year. My confidence would be shot, interest *would lag, the organization would fall apart, and Man In Motion would be remembered as "that thing that was a pretty good idea, but they just never got it together." It was simple, we had to go now or never.*

My anxiousness turned sober as I glanced at the parents of my good friend, Terry Fox. I could not help recalling Terry's fate: the cancer ended his life in the midst of his courageous trek. Thousands and thousands of miles lay before me, sharing the road with speeding cars and trucks, bad weather, the possibility of an accident. Was there a similar fate in store for me?

As I was leaving the auditorium I looked over to see my friend Jim Taylor, with whom I had agreed to collaborate on a book about the Man In Motion World Tour. He was standing near the doorway. He leaned back against the wall with his arms crossed, looking pretty relaxed and confident as I passed. At that moment, my chair's front wheels hit the lip of the door sill, stopping me for a split-second and actually bumping me back slightly. Jim's face seemed clouded with doubt and concern as he walked quickly to my side. He leaned down and whispered, "I hope you do better than that in the Alps, Rick, because a book entitled 'Almost Around the World by Wheelchair' won't sell beans."

Not even underway yet and I was already tired and frustrated; the undertaking seemed so overwhelming, especially with a mere door sill currently blocking my way. I backed up a bit, got a roll at it and cleared the first obstacle.

•

Let's review where you are in the change process. You have identified what it is that you want to change and have cultivated a personal vision of your goal. You have also designed a realistic plan to reach it. Now comes the most challenging part of the process. You must commit to your goal and put your plan into action. At the end of Step #1, we said that you could defer your commitment, if you felt unsure, until you had a chance to create your personal vision and find out, through planning, what you would be getting yourself into. But you can't put it off any longer. Intentions are fine, but commitment and action are what will turn your goal into a reality.

This is the turning point in the process, because without taking action you can never realize your goal. To take action is to actually start your plan in motion. For many people, this is the crucial moment at which their best dreams die—not from action, but inaction. They do not start, they do not step off the edge, and thus, their goals and visions may forever remain unrealized.

Why is this the point at which people have so much difficulty? One explanation is that taking action, by definition, entails venturing into the unknown, and the unknown involves uncertainty. Taking action almost invariably means taking risks because *any* step directed toward reaching your goal is new, toward an unknown, and therefore raises the possibility of failure. Starting is itself a risk, but it is one that you must take if you are ever to achieve your goal. Yes, look before you leap, but leap you must.

Not risking has its benefits. By not risking, you cannot fail. But it is just as certain that if you don't risk, you don't change. If you minimize the risk, then you minimize your potential for gain.

By starting and taking action, you will reap rewards. When you take risks, you automatically break old patterns and open up new possibilities. Through exploring new possibilities, you will have new experiences. Through these new experiences, you are able to discover new things about yourself. You build on each new experience and come to feel differently about yourself as you move closer to your goal.

Principle #1
Take risks despite how you feel.

You may feel completely confident about your ability to take the risks that lie ahead, but even if you don't, you need to take risks despite feeling unsure of yourself. We have found that those who accomplish personal change do so, in large part, because they risk *without* the emotional comfort of feeling 'up' to what they face. In other words, they do not necessarily feel positive when they start. In fact, they often feel the opposite—unprepared, even fearful when initiating action. People who are effective in working with change in their lives take risks, grow and succeed despite being unsure, frightened and less-than-positive at the outset. By acting *despite* these feelings, they move forward in their process of change, and eventually they succeed.

Not only do people skilled in personal change take risks without always feeling up to it emotionally, they also take risks without having a high degree of confidence regarding the outcome. They do not necessarily feel optimistic; they are often unsure whether or not they will succeed. In other words, there are no guarantees, there is no such thing as a 'sure bet', but people risk and succeed nonetheless.

•

When I started the tour, I was never sure that I could actually wheel around the world, but I was sure that I could try. I continually grappled with my fear and was plagued with self-doubt. What would people think of me if I didn't succeed? Would I have to move away and assume a new name? Did I have what it would take? Could I do it? Could anyone do it? Much of the time I simply felt overwhelmed by the immensity of the task that lay ahead and the sheer uncertainty of it all. At times I wondered if I was just plain crazy. I kept asking myself, "What am I doing here?" I felt periodically paralyzed by these feelings, fearful they would sabotage the tour, but despite them, I started. Making that first stroke, just starting, was the biggest risk of all.

•

When you think about it, this is 'true' risk-taking—acting *without* confidence. A risk is not a risk if you are confident of the outcome. Surprisingly, this idea runs counter not only to the self-help literature but also to current psychological theory.

The importance of taking risks in order to achieve success is commonly espoused by self-help advisors. However, the general perspective is that you must develop a positive attitude before you take action—that to get moving and become successful, people need simply set aside or ignore their fears and uncertainties. These advocates seem to be suggesting that you must first talk yourself out of your feelings in order to succeed. Just focus on the positive, we are told. Be optimistic! Don't worry, be happy!

In real life, however, many people are simply unable to change how they feel by merely thinking differently or by forcing a positive attitude. As a result, many people remain stuck in the same old patterns. Others are able to develop a positive frame of mind, but they can only maintain it for short periods. The standard complaint, as with so many weight-loss programs, is that any results achieved are very often short-lived.

We are not denying or ignoring the power of positive thinking, but as presented, the expectation seems quite unrealistic. Thinking does not make it so. The inability to develop or maintain a positive outlook can also deepen existing feelings of failure and inadequacy. Success reported by only a very few people, or results that are short-lived or ineffective, would seem to indicate critical flaws in many of these so-called personal growth formulas.

Likewise, the general consensus among psychologists is that people are more likely to risk when they feel confident that their actions will result in success. Albert Bandura, a prominent psychologist at Stanford University, coined the term "self-efficacy" to refer to people's judgements of their personal capabilities to take effective action. Simply put, self-efficacy is concerned with people's beliefs in their ability to complete successfully a task, such as giving a speech or following an exercise program. According to Bandura, in order for people to achieve their desired goal, they must first believe that they have the ability to be successful. He further states that self-efficacy will affect people's behaviour, the goals they set and the commitment they make to those goals. Those who regard themselves as having little self-efficacy will shy away from risks.

Yet, this does not seem to be the case in people's real-life experiences. In fact, it appears to be just the *opposite*. People who have made changes in their life took risks *despite* a lack of confidence. Action, then, was initiated when people did not believe that they were necessarily going to be successful. They acted, despite the uncertainties—theirs or others'—that surrounded them.

Strategy: Acknowledging Your Feelings

It is essential that you acknowledge and accept your feelings rather than ignore or deny them. What feelings well up inside you when you contemplate taking that first step toward your goal? Write them down in your journal.

Most importantly, you need to act despite your feelings. *Acknowledge your fears, then stride past them!* When you act despite fear and uncertainty, you break away from your pre-existing pattern of behaviour. By persevering (which we will discuss in detail in the next step), you will eventually experience success, and soon find yourself in a position to build on these new experiences. Each achievement, no matter how small, reinforces risk-taking and provides the necessary foundation of incentive, encouragement and experience which enables you to go forward.

Write down how you feel after taking your first step. Do you notice any difference? Which of your old feelings are still with you? What new ones—positive or negative—emerge? Are they telling you something valid, that you need to pay attention to? After all, fear can be a legitimate part of the survival instinct. In Step #5, we will focus on how to deal with the feelings that naturally come to the fore in the process of personal change.

Strategy: Sharing Your Feelings

If you find yourself beset by trepidation, you don't have to suffer in silence and solitude. Now is the time to actively seek out the support and encouragement of others. Friends and family members, mentors and advisors, all stand ready to offer you support. Chances are, many of them have experienced similar feelings when they set out to make changes in their lives. Share your feelings with them. They may be able to offer you a new perspective which will allow you to see your situation in a different light. Don't discount the benefit of simply expressing your feelings to a sympathetic listener; it often seems to lighten the load. Can you identify people you could turn to for support?

Principle #2

Expect the unexpected.

Once you start, changes will occur and things will happen that you cannot anticipate. Therefore, simply starting not only sets the plan in motion but also opens the door to the unpredictable. This is another reason people find it so difficult to start. When you risk, you must expect the unexpected. Confronting the unknown is inevitable.

Recall that, in Step #3, we emphasized the need for your plan to be flexible and adaptable. The same thing applies to your attitude. Once you set the train in motion, be fore-warned that you might have to switch tracks. If you take the attitude from the outset that sometimes you'll have to roll with the punches, you won't feel sandbagged when something you haven't anticipated sneaks up on you.

•

There were times on the tour when circumstance affected our objective, and we needed to respond. En route we had planned to wheel through the Soviet Union, Poland and East Germany, yet the Soviet Union and East Germany refused to grant us the necessary entry visas. We did end up flying to Moscow to meet with disabled athletes, and to have our pic-ture taken on Red Square in front of the Kremlin. But that was it. On the flight back we flushed the toilet over East Germany.

We had also planned to wheel through North Africa, on our way to Sicily and eventually to Rome. But while we were on the road the Italian cruise ship Achille Lauro was hijacked by terrorists, which raised the question of whether it was advisable to enter Italy through Algeria and Tunisia. The Canadian External Affairs Department advised us to change our route. Reluctantly, we complied.

At our current rate, we weren't going to be home in time to finish at EXPO 86. So, did we make that a priority, which would mean skipping Greece, Yugoslavia and the Middle East, or press on with a more realistic finish date, like some-time in November? Racing on our original route to try to keep a date with EXPO 86 was out of the question. And that really ticked me off.

In my heart, I knew that had I not had the dislocated shoulder and the injury to my biceps tendon on my right shoulder I would have been able to do it, and do it with style—70 miles per day, finishing fit and strong. I knew my arms weren't hurting just because of the 70 miles per day. The left shoulder was hurting because of the right shoulder. The right shoulder was hurting because the injury had been there from the beginning.

If I'd been able to start in 1980 or 1981 when I first had the idea, I would have been stronger and more relaxed because I wouldn't have had to concentrate on every stroke lest I aggravated something—we figured I had done about four million strokes by that point. I knew the next part from Poland to Greece was going to be tough. I had to snap myself out of what might have been. I reminded myself of the 7,000 miles in the bank and said, "You know, you're going to finish this thing, no matter how long it takes. So, get to it!"

Principle #3

Analyze the constraints.

You have your goal. You know what you need to do because you have a plan. Now you need to do it. But you find you can't start. What's stopping you from starting? In order to find out, you need to analyze what you see as constraints. This principle is designed to help those of you who truly want to risk, but are stuck in the starting blocks.

To get unstuck, you must understand why you are stuck in the first place. When you are stuck, it is helpful to realize that you tend to do the same things over and over in order to maximize your sense of safety and security, and the predictability of your life or surroundings. You tend to avoid risks, favouring the familiar over changes you fear. As Hamlet suggests, we would "rather bear those ills we have than fly to those we know not of, thus conscience does make cowards of us all."

There are a variety of reasons people find themselves unable to risk. Fearing change is certainly one valid explanation. However, people's inaction is not that simple. We can be constrained from taking risks for a number of reasons. Were it not so, people would read about the importance of risk-taking and just go out and do it.

We have identified three main types of constraints which frequently interfere with risk-taking. These are *circumstances, thoughts* and *feelings*. One or more can constrain you, and they often overlap. Certainly there are other kinds of constraints, but for our purposes we will only address these three main ones.

Circumstances

You may feel constrained from taking risks by your circumstances. You may hear yourself saying things such as, "I can't do it because. . . ." Maybe you may feel restricted by a physical limitation, constrained by a system or an institution. If perhaps you are unemployed and trying to find work, you may find yourself constrained by other people's attitudes. You may be constrained by a lack of education. You may feel limited by a person, as in the case of an unsupportive spouse.

As is often the case, you may have financial constraints. For example, you may want to change careers but feel constrained because of insufficient funds. Getting a more detailed picture of your financial situation can often lead to finding a means of overcoming the problem. For example, going to medical school means a considerable financial investment. In order to obtain the necessary funds, you would need to decide what you are willing to do and to risk to get them. The constraint, however, is not insurmountable or beyond your control.

Some circumstances are fixed, absolute, permanent. They are impossible to change. Others seem that way, but actually are not. Most often we feel blocked by confusing those constraints that are fixed and immutable with those that are not. If, for example, you are blind and you aspire to be a commercial pilot, your vision is an unchangeable constraint. If you are not a natural-born citizen of the United States, you cannot be elected president. If you are a man, you cannot give birth.

However, if you are a woman responsible for raising a family and your goal is to graduate from college, your family responsibilities do not constitute an absolute constraint to your career goal. Family responsibilities may make attending college difficult or even improbable, but not impossible. In such a case, you can decide whether or not you want to overcome the constraint. When you really think about it, there aren't that many absolutes.

Once you learn to distinguish between those circumstances you cannot change and those you can—and learn to act on the latter—a new world of opportunities will open up to you.

•

One day I tried to get my friends organized for a fishing trip, but no one wanted to go. Suddenly, I realized that I was depending too much on others and quickly decided to go by myself. I assembled and packed my gear and drove for over an hour to a fishing spot I had known since my youth. I drove until I arrived at a fence which stood between me and the river. "Well, I've come this far," I thought. "Why should I let this deter me?" I struggled over the fence with my wheelchair and gear. To reach the river I had to go up hill, through a ditch, over another barbed wire fence, through a meadow, and down yet another hill. As I assembled my gear and began to fish, I felt good being able to do it just as I had before. As I sat beside the river, I appreciated my accomplishment. The accomplishment gave additional meaning to a good day.

The fishing, however, was not very good and I decided to try my luck downriver, over another plateau. On the downhill side, I picked up too much speed, caught a wheel in the soft soil and tipped over the embankment into the river, wheelchair and all.

My first thought was "Save yourself," which was brilliant. There wasn't another soul for miles. If I didn't save myself, who would? My next thought, crazily, was "I hope no one's watching." I felt so embarrassed at having been so stupid.

Despite the shock of the cold water and the fear of drowning, I recovered quickly and was able to grasp the side of the embankment, then grabbed my wheelchair before it sank. Slowly, I inched myself out of the water and onto the bank, pulling though the mud and vegetation. Once completely out of the water, I struggled to pull my wheelchair free.

When I finally regained the top of the embankment, righted my wheelchair and settled in, I did so not just with thankfulness and relief, but with an exhilarating sense of independence and accomplishment.

•

Thoughts

A man, having looted a city, was trying to sell an exquisite rug, one of the spoils. "Who will give me 100 pieces of gold for this rug?" he cried throughout the town. A buyer soon approached and the sale was completed. Moments later, a comrade approached the seller. "Why did you not ask more for that priceless rug?" he asked. "Is there any number higher than 100?" replied the seller.

In this simple but elegant Sufi teaching story you can see how the rugseller was confined by his beliefs and attitudes. He was limited and constrained by what he thought was possible.

Your thoughts can stop you from taking risks because they can limit your awareness and, therefore, impede your actions. As in the case of the rugseller, they can also create an insensitivity to new information. The end result is that your options and choices are limited because you can't conceive of them. Or, you don't learn new skills or abilities because you aren't aware they exist.

In the fall of 1976, I enrolled at the University of British Columbia, not in Physical Education as I had wanted, but in a first year Arts program. It was that or nothing. The admissions board obviously didn't like the chances of a guy in a wheelchair trying for a Bachelor of Physical Education degree. Apparently, since it had never been done, it could not be done. Maybe in second year we could discuss it, they said, if I was still interested. Finally, UBC relented and I entered the School of Physical Education for second year, thanks mainly to the tireless efforts of my advisor.

•

The admissions board did not think it was possible for a man in a wheelchair to achieve a degree in physical education, so no provisions had been made for evaluating such a request. Challenging their restrictive thinking expanded their ideas of what was possible.

People are also stopped from taking risks because they think of themselves as incompetent or inadequate. For some, this sense of incompetence may be confined to specific areas such as career or relationships. In these situations people may think they lack the necessary skills or abilities for effective action, and, consequently, they don't act. For others, a sense of incompetence may be generalized to all aspects of their lives. These people tend to think they are unable or incapable of getting what they want or need in the world, and therefore give up before they start.

Whether the sense of incompetence is induced through circumstances or has a more enduring, deeper origin, the net effect is to limit the person. New experiences and opportunities are left untapped. Risks and challenges are avoided. Skills and abilities remain undeveloped. Henry Ford once said: "If you think you can do it, you're right. If you think you *can't* do it, you're still right."

•

After my accident, I felt stripped of my previous skills and abilities; I felt completely incompetent. In that state of mind, I was very apprehensive about returning to school. Once, I was an all-star athlete, and now I was a 'cripple'.

The worst part of the day was P.E. class. I forced myself to go back into that gym, both hating and longing to be there. Such a short time before, I virtually lived for sports. In gym, all the sparkle of my old life confronted the bleakness of my current situation. This conflict between old aspirations and present realities began to change when the coach of my old volleyball team asked me to be his assistant. "Why don't you come out and help me coach these guys?" he asked. When I said that I couldn't, he looked at me and said "Why not?" It was a good question. Fortunately, he persisted and I ran out of excuses. I finally decided to risk accepting his offer.

It took a while to feel comfortable because it was a new role in sports for me, one I had not envisioned before. Yet, it offered its own satisfactions and allowed me to participate in a different way, like a new door opening when before they had all seemed to be locked tight.

•

Feelings

You can also be constrained from taking risks by your feelings. The most common feeling that gets in the way of risk-taking is a weak or even absent sense of self-worth. People who do not believe in themselves do not act because they have come to feel powerless and trapped. They frequently lack motivation, become apathetic and complacent, accepting what is, rather than trying to change.

At the core of a weak sense of self-worth is the overriding feeling that the 'real' self is worthless, unacceptable and, therefore, must be covered up and hidden. People who lack self-worth have a tendency to not act on authentic, meaningful motives. That which is most meaningful to them—

whether it's a feeling, a goal or a thought—is not divulged, but instead is hidden away. It is not acted upon and, consequently, is not made a reality in their life.

People feel a sense of worthlessness for many different reasons. From our perspective, the reason, regardless of its validity, should not prevent you from taking action. You don't have to have a strong sense of self-worth to risk and succeed. However, you must be willing to push through the discomfort and take the risk despite these feelings. This is what counts—taking action despite how you feel about yourself. It is through the experience of taking risks that you will naturally enhance your self-worth.

Rick's overwhelming feelings of worthlessness were the direct result of his injury. Within seconds, his life changed forever. Many of his invaluable physical abilities were gone and, with them, his sense of worth. This loss was immobilizing, especially when it came to romance. Although he sometimes flirted with student nurses in the hospital, he was convinced that dating would never be possible, and that all he could do was dream.

•

Even after I was released from the hospital, I still avoided dating; I felt terribly insecure and feared girls would reject me. Rejection would certainly reinforce my feeling that I was not worthy. After all, no girl in her right mind would want to go out with me unless she felt sorry for me.

I was too unattractive for dating. How would a girl feel about being seen with someone in a wheelchair? I simply didn't measure up any more. I was no longer an athlete. I couldn't drive a car. I couldn't even dance. All the things that other kids did together, both socially and recreationally, were presently beyond my abilities. There were far more 'couldn'ts' than 'coulds'. Romantically, I lived a vicarious life by giving advice to my lovelorn friends.

Much to my surprise, a girl in one of my classes began smiling at me. One day after class, she asked me out on a date. Despite my suspicion that she merely felt sorry for me, I accepted. It was a huge risk for two reasons. First, there was the fear of rejection, then the hurt should I find out that she did indeed ask me only out of pity. It would have just reinforced what I was already feeling about myself; it would have been very difficult to overcome.

•

Fortunately, Rick's fears were unfounded and he dated this particular girl for more than three months. Taking this first risk gave him the opportunity to see that there might be more to attractiveness than his physical capabilities. With the boost to his self-esteem this experience provided, he next summoned up the courage to ask another girl out despite his reservations. The potential benefits of having a relationship began to outweigh the possibility of being rejected. He asked, she accepted, and they stayed together for over three years; Patti Lueke became a significant influence in Rick's life.

Strategy: Breaking through Constraints

Are you feeling constrained from taking risks by circumstances, thoughts or feelings? If so, describe these constraints specifically and clearly in your journal. Determine if each constraint is changeable or unchangeable.

If, after analyzing the constraint, you find that it is unchangeable, then you may need to go back to Step #1 and set another goal or modify your present one. Trying to change the unchangeable is a waste of your valuable time and energy.

If, on the other hand, the constraint is changeable, then you need to analyze it carefully to determine specifically what needs to be addressed to resolve the problem. Is it your thinking that needs adjusting? Or, is it a feeling that is getting in your way?

For example, Chris feels constrained from changing jobs. She decides to stay on in a boring but secure job instead of taking a new but challenging one that is available to her. After analyzing her situation she realizes that the constraint is changeable—it comes from within, in the form of confining thoughts and feelings.

She is able to identify her internal constraints as a sense of inadequacy and a fear of failing. She decides to take steps to resolve the situation. If she doesn't, she knows that she will be disappointed in herself and live to regret her decision. The first step she takes is to talk to her friends to gain their emotional support, and to get their opinions about the new job and her ability to handle it. Then, she discusses her job performance with her current employer in order to elicit some direct, objective feedback about her skills and abilities. Finally, she approaches the new employer and requests more information about the job, as well as objective information about why she is being considered for the position. With this bolstered strength and objective input, Chris feels less stuck and is able to reconsider her decision.

Now that you have identified what needs to change, you will need to take the necessary steps to resolve the problem. You may find that it cannot be resolved that easily. If this is the case, you may need to acknowledge the confining thought or feeling and, using Principles #1 and #2, take risks anyway.

Getting Out of the Starting Gate

Richard Warren Sears's entrepreneurial goal was simple. He wanted to bring consumer goods that were easily available in the city to rural America. Early in this effort, Sears toured a clothing factory with its owner. He explained that he wanted to place an order for 10,000 pairs of men's pants and sell them through his Sears, Roebuck and Co. catalogue. How soon could the owner fill the order? The man was shocked; Sears's request represented a significant percentage of his factory's entire annual production.

"Mr. Sears, wouldn't it be better if you first tried selling, say, a thousand pair in your catalogue," the man said, urging caution. "No," said Sears, "I've already sold them." Sears's risk-taking style of business, such as selling 10,000 pairs of pants he did not have and might not find, had caused the departure of his first business partner, Alvah Roebuck. Haunted by fears that Sears's take-no-prisoners approach would ruin him financially, Roebuck sold his share in the young company for $25,000. Fourteen years later, Richard Sears—the consummate salesman—sold his share in the giant firm for $10 million.

Keeping in mind the principles outlined above, and after considering the things that are getting in your way, you must now take your first risk and start. Remember that some people will find this step easier than others, depending on their skill level and their previous experience with risks. Taking risks was not a particularly new experience for Rick. He was a risk-taker long before his accident; it was his nature. However, even if you aren't a risk-taker, despite your apprehension, you need to become one in order to achieve your goal—in order to achieve personal change.

Summary

Step #4

Taking Risks

Principles

#1. Take risks despite how you feel.
#2. Expect the unexpected.
#3. Analyze the constraints.

STEP #5

EMBRACING FEELINGS

*I came to recognize that the driving force
behind my reactions was fear, frustration and an
overwhelming sense of responsibility.*

We had started the tour before we were ready. We were making a lot of mistakes. Things just weren't happening, and we were paying for it. As well, I was dealing with my own anger, frustration and disappointment. I worked myself into quite a frenzy. Every time a mistake was made, I ended up spending too much time and wasting a lot of energy being overzealous or overly concerned with every single problem. I was being eaten up with anger. I was sniping at everyone, creating a negative atmosphere. This kind of destructive behaviour was destined to get us into trouble.

As we got closer to Texas, a few weeks into the tour, things came to a head. I asked Tim, our road manager, to do something—my way. He did it his way and I was furious. We were inside the motorhome during a break; I yelled at him and he yelled at me—we just blew up. I abruptly left the vehicle and wheeled away.

When the dust settled, I started to recognize that if I was going to continue to expect everyone to do everything my way, I might as well do it all myself. Clearly, that wasn't going to work. What I needed to do was to cut everybody more slack. I knew I wasn't handling things well. Sometimes I expected too much or became unreasonable and too blunt in my demands. I also had to work on being more understanding and more diplomatic. I needed to have more faith in others' abilities, and let them make their own mistakes and continue to learn about themselves. After all, wasn't that my philosophy?

I also knew I had to uncover the source of my feelings. If I didn't, my anger was going to drive everyone away. I came to recognize that the driving force behind my reactions was fear,

*frustration and an overwhelming sense of responsibility. I had
started this thing and nothing was happening, or at least it
seemed that way to me. I realized that I had to channel my
energy more productively and translate my anger into a more
positive force. I decided to search for new ways to work better
together as a team and to organize the project more effectively. In effect, the things that were not happening and the
mistakes that were being made began to intensify my efforts
to prevent them from recurring.*

●

Although strong feelings will likely accompany each step of
the change process, those that significantly hinder movement toward your goal are most likely to first arise during
the risk-taking step. As you continue along the path toward
your goal, strong feelings will inevitably be triggered because
you are entering into unknown, uncharted territory. By
feelings, we are referring to emotional responses such as
fear, anger, anxiety, depression and frustration.

As you go through the change process, you need to learn
to attend to what you are feeling, not just to what you are
thinking and doing. Otherwise, it's like working out and
neglecting a key muscle group. You must also learn to be
honest with yourself about your feelings. If you don't, it's
like lying to a doctor about a health problem. It's difficult
for your doctor to treat the problem if she doesn't know all
the symptoms.

Your feelings are an important source of knowledge and
wisdom about yourself that cannot be found anywhere
else—not in books, not in audiotapes, not in lectures, nor
from other people. This inner resource is invaluable and
provides you with a personal guide to successful goal-
directed action. Learning to understand, accept and benefit
from these feelings in an effort to maximize success is the
focus of this step.

The Neglect of Feelings

The whole subject of personal change, if not examined carefully, invites us to pay attention to the **action** involved and how that action unfolds, and to neglect the **feelings** that precede, accompany, follow or maintain that action.

Such has been the case in the self-help movement. The general trend has been to focus on *thoughts* and their relationship to action. A vast array of approaches and strategies has been developed for helping people to think differently, to alter their beliefs and attitudes. But, by focusing entirely on thoughts, the importance of *feelings* and their role in personal change has been largely ignored.

Emotions not only are de-emphasized, they are actively devalued and discounted. Over and over again, we are given a clear message that emotions are 'unfortunate evils' with which we all must contend, a negative force that impedes success and must be driven out. The message, stated either directly or indirectly, is that we must be rational—not emotional—if we are to be successful in achieving our goals. We are instructed to avoid emotional responses in favour of simply *thinking* our way through situations. We are urged to 'rid ourselves' of emotions by controlling and mastering them. We are told to ignore our feelings by simply substituting positive thoughts.

Yet, whenever we do not succeed in making a personal change, it is almost invariably feelings that trip us up. Feelings can no more be set aside in a successful attempt at change than can thoughts or actions. When people follow advice to disregard or downplay the importance of feelings in personal change, is it any wonder that they have difficulty maintaining that change, or, that the results do not last?

We have found that people identified and experienced feelings as integral parts of successful personal change. As feelings were acknowledged and addressed throughout the process, successful and lasting personal change was achieved.

Therefore, from our perspective, for there to be significant and enduring change, people must address all three of their human capacities: the ability to think, to act *and to feel*. When we seek to redress the balance between our thoughts and feelings, and their respective relationships to action, we begin a more complete approach to personal change. Only then may we see the results that we expect and desire.

Here's a familiar scenario. George desperately wanted to leave his job. He worked at the bank and over time thought about all the logical, rational reasons for leaving. However, a change would involve a significant risk—to walk away from the secure job and the steady income. When confronted with the possibility that he might not easily find a new job, his fear overwhelmed him. He was convinced that he would lose his home. Time and again he had started a job search—even received some encouraging initial responses from prospective employers—but always his fear was great enough to stop him from following through. He had failed to deal with the emotional part of achieving his goal.

Principle #1

Accept your negative feelings.

As you start to take risks, you will probably be comfortable with the positive feelings that arise, such as satisfaction and gratification. However, you may be hindered by the feelings we generally regard as negative such as fear, anger, anxiety, depression and frustration. Why? Because they feel bad—it's as simple as that.

Feeling badly, however, is not necessarily a bad thing. Feeling badly is simply a message from the inside that something is wrong. Difficult emotions are red flags or internal signals that call our attention to exactly what we need to do differently in order to move forward toward our goal. In this way, by taking 'counsel' of our feelings, we can actually use our difficult emotions as 'advisors' that point us in a new direction.

To successfully address difficult emotions, then, you need to adjust your approach to them. You must recognize that they are not to be feared or avoided, but instead, they must be respected and attended to, just like the positive ones. You need to learn to listen to them and convert them into constructive action. A crucial point here is that we're not talking about substituting a positive feeling for a negative one, but instead, *listening* to the message being sent by the negative feeling and *responding* to the message by taking appropriate and constructive action.

You might find this troublesome in the beginning because more often than not we tend to shy away from fear, anger, frustration—the difficult feelings. After all, isn't it far more enjoyable to imagine what you would do with the lottery winnings than to deal with your fear of being unemployed?

•

I was always the kind of kid who, when the teacher asked questions, would bury my head in my notebook and start to scribble like I was busy, hoping she wouldn't ask me. I was extremely shy and afraid of talking in groups. On this one day, while I was a student at the University of British Columbia, I remember being asked by my professor to come in and talk to my peers about my accident, about my disability and about sports for athletes with disabilities. I almost declined, but then I felt embarrassed; why shouldn't I be willing to speak about something I felt passionately about, and share my ideas? So I went in and made my presentation despite great fear and feeling highly self-conscious. It was extremely painful, and I was very nervous. But by facing my fear, and working through it, I started to feel more comfortable about speaking in groups.

When it came time to raise seed money for the Man In Motion World Tour, I remember the time I was first called upon to speak to potential sponsors at the Point Grey Golf Club. Here again were those old familiar feelings—dry mouth, rapid heart rate, heart bulging into my throat. What saved me then, as before, was the belief that if I were just myself—speaking from the heart, being authentic—then they really couldn't ask for anything more. I was Rick Hansen, and no one could take that away from me. So I made my pitch, despite feeling awkward, self-conscious and anxious.

By the time I came home from the Man In Motion World Tour, I had given thousands of speeches, interviews and presentations. I had grown to feel pretty comfortable doing so— it actually became automatic. But then IBM asked me to deliver a 45-minute address to their employees, and the same old anxiety and fear invaded my mind and heart. But this time I recognized it for what it was, and I knew that painful as it might be it wouldn't prevent me from getting my message across.

•

Strategy: Acknowledging Your Feelings

The following exercise is designed to help you learn to acknowledge your feelings and attend to them in a constructive way.

First, listen carefully and pay attention to what you are feeling in your body. For example, "I feel tense" or "My heart is racing."

Second, identify the feeling that underlies the body experience. "I am tense because I feel inadequate in this situation."

Third, pause, step back, and draw out the personal meaning of this feeling. "I feel inadequate about this situation because I have never done anything like this before."

Fourth, face the total meaning of the feeling. Assess its accuracy and usefulness. That is, question the meaning of the feeling. (Am I really inadequate?)

Fifth, respond to the feeling. For example, if you have concluded that you are, in fact, inadequate to the task at hand, then you will need to take steps to develop the skills you need to go forward. If you are not inadequate, but you feel inadequate, you need to acknowledge this feeling. Don't try to talk yourself out of it or ignore it. Recognize and accept it, but act despite it. Through taking action, feelings of adequacy will naturally develop.

Sixth, if there is nothing you can do to respond to the feeling, then try to convert it to a positive force. For example, fear or anger can be very functional if it is converted into determination. Depression can actually propel you into a period of introspection which can lead to a pronounced inner change or decision.

When you take these steps, each emotional response becomes an opportunity to sharpen awareness and to clarify direction. By tuning in to your inner experience, you make available valuable information that guides and directs you in the pursuit of your goal—information that cannot be found anywhere else.

•

Without a doubt, there were some challenging times on the road in terms of my relationship with Amanda. She was my intermediary, always the buffer between me and the crew or me and the home office. She was also my friend, the only one who allowed me to really be myself, because I was on show pretty much 99 percent of the time. There were sides of me that I needed to express and Amanda was my sounding-board. In that role, she often bore the brunt of the negative stuff.

I was overly sensitive, and there were times when I felt she was taking the side of the crew members without seeing my perspective. I felt so isolated and would end up lashing out in frustration. Once, during dinner one evening in New Zealand, we had a blow-up and threw salad all over each other. Stupid. But it did bring us to an important decision point in our relationship. I knew then just how important my relationship with Amanda was to me.

What I finally had to recognize was that part of the problem was the association of the negative emotions with someone I loved. I had to recognize that it was okay to feel that way about someone whom you love; you could feel both positively and negatively. At the same time, I had to recognize that part of the frustration I was feeling was a sense of loneliness. Here was the one person I thought could understand and relate to me, and she was expressing a difference of opinion. The anger was coming from the loneliness and my deep sense of isolation. I realized that there were times when Amanda would disagree with me, and she deserved to be respected for that. It didn't mean that she didn't understand—there's a big difference.

Principle #2

Uncover your emotional blocks.

What happens if difficult emotions arise, but you are unable to move past them and they do prevent you from taking action? The first step in moving beyond them is to uncover how and what you are doing to block yourself. There are four basic ways that you may be getting in your own way.

Avoiding

If you are blocked, you may be avoiding a difficult feeling. People tend to avoid feelings which threaten to overwhelm them. When people feel overwhelmed, they become immobilized and are unable to act. For example, a fear of failing may be so intense that it causes you to avoid taking risks such as applying for a challenging, new job. Feelings of inadequacy or worthlessness can result in inaction through avoiding new experiences and favouring the familiar. When you have the emotional experience of feeling 'stuck', you are more than likely avoiding a difficult feeling of some kind.

●

We were in Czechoslovakia when Tim, our road manager, decided to leave the tour. I was devastated. The deal had always been that we would start the tour together and we would finish together—all for one; one for all. In the end it was his health. I understood and respected his decision to leave because he had given all he could, but I couldn't shake the feeling of disappointment that he would not finish with us.

There was so much to attend to on the road that I wasn't really able to come to grips with losing Tim until a few months later. He had come back to visit us in New Zealand and I was still allowing my feelings about his leaving to get in the way of our friendship. About four months after he left, I was finally able to deal with my emotions about his departure from the tour. I was able to understand that underlying my disappointment and perhaps a feeling of abandonment, was the pain of losing a part of the original dream. As well, I felt guilty and responsible that I had not given more support to Tim through his struggle on the tour.

Tim and I had promised that our friendship would not interfere with the tour, and that the tour would not interfere with our friendship. Finally, as I continued to sort out my feelings, it seemed clear that I had lost sight of the second part of that equation. Also, I realized that part of the original dream—that everyone would hang in there for two years— was unrealistic. It was the cause, the round-the-world tour, that was more important than any one of us being there to see it through.

I also discovered that my guilt about not supporting Tim as I might have was based on an unrealistic expectation of my strength and energy during the tour. As I was able to get some perspective, I knew that there was no way I could have given him more; I was just barely surviving myself. I decided that any time, any place, with anyone, you're going to feel good and you're going to feel bad. It's important to understand both . . . perhaps the bad feelings require even more understanding.

●

Numbing

One form of avoiding is numbing. Numbing refers to a closing off or a shutting down of your feelings. Numbing involves actively suppressing those feelings that are perceived to be unacceptable or 'toxic' in some way. Numbing is a way of reacting that is believed to provide self-protection and a means of escape from difficult feelings. A signal that you may be using this strategy is the excessive use of external aids such as drugs or alcohol, or behaviours such as overeating. 'Workaholism' is one such behaviour that appears deceptively healthy. From the outside it seems that the person is a hard worker, a good employee, a successful businessperson. In truth, he or she may simply be avoiding certain feelings with the constant distraction of work.

Although numbing may act as a pain killer in the short run, in the end it is harmful because it keeps important emotional information beyond your reach. If you are numb to the pain and its origin, you are without the key information you need to address the pain. Numbing shuts out toxic feelings, but it also shuts you in. It becomes a trap from which you may see no escape. If you are feeling 'nothing' or 'kind of dead inside', then you are probably numbing a difficult feeling.

Denying

If you are blocked, you may be trying to deny a difficult feeling. You may be feeling one way, but trying to convince yourself or others that you feel just the opposite. For example, you may feel negatively about your job, but try to convince yourself that you really feel positively about it. Max knows that he is underpaid in his job, but he tries to convince himself to feel or think differently by focusing on its medical and pension benefits and his two-week paid vacation. That is easier than facing his anger and frustration about being underpaid.

By denying your true feelings you risk preventing yourself from taking action to change the situation. Until you address the 'real' feeling, you remain blocked or paralyzed. Eventually, the difficult emotion will rise up again and again with ever-increasing intensity until you finally attend to it. When you have the emotional experience of feeling trapped, you are more than likely denying a difficult feeling of some kind.

•

Romance on the road. Not altogether bad, but if the road stretches on ahead for two years, there can certainly be problems. It had been virtually impossible for Amanda and me to spend much time cementing our new-found relationship, despite the fact that we were spending 24 hours of every day together. New relationships are hard enough, but trying to wheel around the world and be a 'normal' couple at the same time was almost laughable . . . now.

One day Amanda announced that she was going to go to Tallahassee, Florida, with Tim in advance of the road crew and that we'd all meet up at the hotel at the end of the day. She hadn't had a break in a long while and it was a good opportunity for her and Tim to get some other work done and take a breather at the same time. My response? First-class jerk.

As soon as they left I began to feel more tense and irrita-
ble. I was looking for any little thing to bitch at. It got worse
and worse right up to the point where I was greeted enthusi-
astically by Tim and Amanda at the hotel. I glared at
Amanda and wheeled past her and into Tim's room. I'd asked
him to change the pushrims of a backup set of wheels and
now I demanded to see them. They hadn't been changed. I
blew up at Tim, letting out all the frustrations of the day. Tim
tried gamely to tell me that he had worked on the chair all
day and that he was going to finish working on the rims that
evening. I wasn't listening. I stormed out of the room.

Clearly, I wasn't upset about rims, wheels, Florida or people
taking a break. The root of the problem—my problem—was
my insecurity about my new relationship with Amanda. I was
simply jealous of her and Tim spending time together and I let
it get the best of me. As I remained in denial of this powerful
feeling, I continued to unintentionally create tension and
disharmony in connection with whomever Amanda would
spend time with. In addition to feeling jealous and insecure, I
realized that I feared losing Amanda because I wasn't in a
position to properly develop a normal relationship. In time, as
our relationship evolved and we were able to bond more
closely, I felt more secure and the problem resolved itself.

•

Misreading the meaning

If you are blocked by a difficult feeling, you may be mis-
reading the *meaning* of the feeling. Feelings can take many
forms. Whether the feeling is constructive or destructive
seems to depend upon the meaning we give to it. For
example, you may feel immobilized with frustration. If you
use the strategy offered in Principle #1 to attend to this
feeling, you may draw out the meaning beneath the feeling
of frustration. You may discover that the frustration indicates that you are doing something that isn't working and

you simply need to adjust your actions accordingly.

If you take the time to listen to these feelings and understand what they are trying to tell you, then you can work toward finding a direct and constructive means of expression for them.

Strategy: Unlocking the Blocks

If you are experiencing difficult feelings and they are preventing you from taking action, you need first to identify how and what you are doing to block yourself. Using the four basic categories above to help you, write your insights down in your journal. Write down whatever you discover, even if it does not fit into one of our categories. The aim is to sharpen your awareness about how you are getting in your own way.

The purpose of the next exercise is to help you unlock the block you have identified. It involves uncovering the feeling that is preventing you from reaching your goal. This exercise has been adapted from a self-help technique called "focusing" that was introduced in 1978 by psychologist Eugene T. Gendlin.

Focusing is generally used as a problem-solving technique. For our purposes, we are applying the technique to specific feelings that become problematic as you take action toward your goal. Focusing is especially well-suited to uncovering the personal meaning associated with our feelings.

Preparing: The first step is to get physically comfortable and relaxed. Turn your attention away from the external world and focus inside yourself. Silence usually facilitates this transition.

Experiencing: The next step is to identify the specific emotion that is getting in your way. If it's a lack of emotion that is getting in the way, focus on that feeling—the 'emptiness' or 'deadness'. If more than one emotion is a problem, focus on the one that seems most important. Get a sense of what the emotion feels like. Take the time to fully *experience* the bodily sensations that are involved. Listen, feel and sense the emotion. Try not to get caught up in the 'noise'—distracting thoughts—that likely come to mind first. You are not seeking to analyze the emotion or uncover its cause. *You are seeking the 'felt sense,' the sense of what the whole emotion feels like.*

For example, think of two people who play major roles in your life. Let's refer to these two people as Gretchen and Rob. You could probably come up with literally hundreds of bits of data to describe them—what they look like, their personality traits, their likes and dislikes, how you met, how they speak, their annoying habits and so on.

Now, let your attention dwell on Gretchen, on the overall sense you have of her. All the hundreds of bits of data that you have stored up in your head about her do not come to you one-by-one in the form of individual thoughts. Instead, they are all experienced simultaneously as a single 'felt sense', or an 'essence' if you will. Now, shift your focus onto Rob, and the overall sense you have of him. Notice the entirely different sense you have. Go back and forth and notice the difference in the felt sense between the two.

Labelling: Now, try to find a word or an image that best captures the *quality* of this felt sense. You are trying to find an accurate label for the core of what you feel. You may come up with words such as angry or inadequate, a phrase such as "wound up tight," or an image such as a rope tied in a knot. Don't stay with the conventional labels that will inevitably come to mind first. Persist until some more personal meaning emerges.

It's kind of like playing the children's game where the one who knows where the object is hidden says "cold, colder, freezing cold" to indicate when you're going in the wrong direction and "warm, warmer, hot" when you're going in the right direction. This time you're playing the game with yourself, listening to your own sense of getting closer and closer to the right label.

At this point, you may begin to notice that you feel differently from what you expected when you started. Pay attention to anything, regardless of how small or subtle it feels, that is accompanied by a body sensation or shift. When you hit upon the right label you may feel a slight release or relief in your body. There is a physical sense of 'rightness', of being a good fit. Discard anything else. Listen only to what your body tells you about how the label you've chosen matches the felt sense, not what your mind tells you to think. Make whatever adjustments you need to improve the match. When you do find the right label, the felt sense stirs and you will experience a small shift in your body that indicates that it is the right label.

Resonating: This step involves trying the label on for size. Does it fit? Does it feel right? Is there a good match between the two? Take time to go back and forth or resonate between the felt sense and the label to ensure its fit. The process of resonating can often result in insight or a new understanding of the emotion.

Listening: The next step is to draw out the personal meaning of the felt sense. You ask the felt sense what it is. If your felt sense was 'inadequate', ask yourself, "What is it about this problem that makes me feel so inadequate?" Stay with the felt sense as you ask the question. Answers from your mind will come quickly. Just let those answers go by. Answers from your body or your felt sense will feel different, and there will be a distinct body shift or sensation as the answer emerges. Once a more accurate, individualistic meaning is uncovered, movement is unlocked.

If the meaning does not emerge, try asking these other questions: What is the worst of this feeling? Or, what is the part of this that makes me feel the most inadequate? What does the felt sense need? What should happen?

Receiving: The next step is to be open and willing to receive the meaning that emerges. Sometimes you may not like the answer that comes to you, but you must be willing to face it in order to move through it.

Responding: Once you know what you are dealing with, you are in a better position to decide what to do about it. In addition to insight and new understanding, the possibilities for action will become evident. In other words, now that you know what you need to do in order to address the feeling, the last step is to do it. Convert your insights into a constructive action plan.

Keep in mind that you may not achieve instant results from this exercise. Like any skill, it will get better with practice.

If you have difficulty with anything, it will likely be with identifying your 'felt sense'. Here's one more example to help you clarify the concept. As golfers tee off, there is no way that they can think simultaneously about all the details that go into that one moment when they feel 'ready' to take their swing. Instead, a golfer gets ready by positioning and re-positioning the whole body—eyes, arms, hands and feet—until one position signals, "I am ready. This feels right."

Here's an illustration of the technique.

Let's imagine Karen, an executive whose goal is to get a promotion. In the past, Karen has been unsuccessful in achieving this goal largely because of her inability to produce reports on time. Toward the end of the fiscal year a particularly important report is expected, and with its successful and timely completion there exists a possible promotion for Karen. The deadline approaches and she sees herself lagging behind once again. She begins to panic and feels stuck.

As she begins the focusing technique, she comes up with the old, familiar perspectives on her problem—"If they would just give me more time, I could get this done." As she tries to put aside these typical judgements, she becomes aware of just how miserable she feels. She attends to these overall feelings with the first labels that come to mind. She feels annoyed with her boss and then helpless to change the situation. As she pushes beyond these initial reactions, she notices a tightening in her chest and a discomfort in her stomach. She recognizes these body sensations as fear. She feels increasingly edgy as she senses the presence of the fear. She imagines herself running away, but never able to escape from an unidentified pursuer.

She keeps asking herself, "What am I so afraid of?" The answer finally emerges, "I could lose my job." Then things begin to fall into place. She remembers times in the past when she was unwilling to perform for fear of being judged to have done a bad job. At those times, she found safety in just not doing her work because then at least what she did do could not be criticized. It becomes clear to her that she is doing the very same thing in not working on the report.

At that point, she realizes that it is she, herself, who is responsible for not getting those past promotions. She now knows that she must do something different in order to avoid history repeating itself. She writes out all the steps she needs to take in order to finish the report and a timeline for each step, then knuckles down to the task.

•

Let's summarize. This chapter is designed to help you learn to identify and effectively address the emotions that naturally arise as you take action to realize your goal. As you work toward your goal, it is essential to experience, express and understand the individual, personal meaning of your feelings. No one else can do this for you because your emotional experience is subjective and, therefore, unique.

Once the meaning is clear, you are in a position to address your feelings. The way the feeling is understood then has implications for what action to take. By listening and responding to your feelings, you not only increase awareness, you provide yourself with important self-direction that is not available through any other means.

Sharpening awareness about your feelings has other significant benefits which become apparent over time. Discovering and addressing your 'real' feelings promotes genuineness and authenticity. As your authentic self emerges, you are more free to explore and clarify those activities and relationships that you find to be personally meaningful. By addressing your real feelings, you are declaring your own self-worth, valuing yourself and your feelings. Such qualities improve your relationship not only with yourself, but with others as well. As you become more in tune with your real feelings and therefore your 'real' self, there is a sense of deep, personal satisfaction. When you are able to be more authentic you will experience a revitalization of your life. As one person who successfully transformed her life said, "It's a revolutionary act to be yourself."

Summary

Step #5

Embracing Feelings

Principles

#1. Accept your negative feelings.
#2. Uncover your emotional blocks.

STEP #6

ACTIVELY STRIVING

*The rain mixed with sleet, then snow, and it was
fast becoming difficult to wheel.
At that point, I wondered if I could even finish the
day, let alone the tour.*

By the second day on the road, I was completely overwhelmed by doubt and uncertainty. I had developed tendinitis in my wrists, elbows and shoulders as a result of 70 miles of wheeling into 60 mile-per-hour headwinds with the temperature hovering near freezing.

The rain mixed with sleet, then snow, and it was fast becoming difficult to wheel. The wind—how I'd already come to hate it—added significant resistance. The slush from the asphalt carried along the tire treads and slopped over my hands. It was becoming almost impossible to grip the pushrims hard enough for an effective stroke. Really unbelievable.

At that point, I wondered if I could even finish the day, let alone finish the tour. Alone with the cold and my thoughts, the day had become a series of moment-to-moment decisions about whether I could, or even should continue.

I rolled slowly to the motorhome for a break, soaking wet and freezing cold. I crawled to my bed in the back of the vehicle and reluctantly put ice packs on my shoulders, elbows and wrists. I just lay there, completely overwhelmed by the enormous problems of the tour stretched out before me. I kept saying to myself, "You don't know what you've gotten yourself into, Rick—you'd better think about it. Maybe you should bail out now." Lying there cold and miserable, I thought seriously about quitting.

A few things stopped me. I reminded myself of my dream. I focused on the commitment that I had made. I thought about Terry Fox and how his quest had ended: he hadn't given up—his body just quit on him. I believed that there would be no shame in walking away from the tour if I honestly had no *regrets. But once the fatigue and the physical discomfort were gone, would I regret quitting? I didn't want to be sitting around with my friends ten years later saying, "If only I could have wheeled around the world." So, I asked myself if I had one more stroke left in me. The answer came back, "Yes."*

I think I literally talked myself out of that nice warm motorhome and into that cold, steel wheelchair; I put on those wet, slimy gloves and once more pushed away from the protection and comfort of the motorhome. My first stroke was greeted by a hard, gusting rain. I took a second stroke, then another, and another. Each series of strokes led to one mile and then to another. That led to getting through half a day, and by the end of the afternoon, I felt one step closer to victory. By nightfall, it was difficult to imagine that just a few hours earlier I had thought about quitting.

•

As you carry out your plan and take risks, you will be actively striving toward your goal. You can set a goal, design a plan and even take risks, but if you don't sustain the action you will never reach your objective.

Sustaining goal-directed action involves two kinds of striving. The first kind of striving entails exerting effort in a concentrated, focused way. Through your efforts you learn that things do not happen effortlessly or magically. You realize that hard work and focused effort are what make things happen. When you work hard and discover that getting what you want is largely in your own hands and not external to yourself, you feel empowered. You expand your sense of your own capabilities.

When you make things happen rather than let them happen to you, you develop a sense of control over your own life. This sense of control helps you feel more passionate about your life because you realize that you have the power to shape its course. The act of striving provides great personal satisfaction and a sense of pride in yourself that is highly motivating. It also provides you with a built-in strategy for getting what you want that, in turn, can be applied to other areas of your life.

The second kind of striving targets obstacles. As you forge ahead, you will inevitably encounter obstacles en route to your goal. Your courage, endurance and energy will most probably be challenged. In undertaking any worthwhile change, you inevitably undergo periods of considerable struggle. Obstacles are normal and to be expected. Learning to handle them is an essential part of learning about effective personal change.

Obstacles come in many forms. They dwell within us as self-defeating **attitudes** (fear of failure) and in self-defeating **behaviours** (losing focus). Or they are found externally in the form of **setbacks** (loss of a job) or changes in **circumstances** (disability or the death of a family member).

Whether we encounter obstacles on the inside or the outside, the overall strategy for dealing with them is the same—*you must actively strive with determination and perseverance in the face of these constraints.* The obstacle, in itself, is not the problem. The problem is how you manage the obstacle and meet the challenges that are presented.

By successfully managing obstacles as they arise, you will soon discover that they represent opportunities from which to learn rather than events to be feared. Once we face and overcome obstacles, we 'detoxify' them. We learn that they do not kill us, but in fact, they can make us stronger and wiser.

Principle #1

Recognize that change is cyclic.

As we pointed out at the start of this book, the process of change does not usually involve a steady, smooth, upward movement. Rather, it is composed of peaks and valleys with varying levels of intensity. The peaks reflect the accomplishment of tasks and movement forward. The valleys reflect the obstacles you face along the way. Contrary to what you may think, the valleys also represent movement forward. The difference is that the peaks feel like the high points and the valleys feel like the low points. A mighty ocean wave swells to a peak, then falls, perhaps suddenly, into a trough before rising once again to a peak, and so on and on. Yet the wave retains its energy as it rolls relentlessly onward.

Be prepared to encounter both the peaks and valleys as you strive toward your goal. Anticipating them and knowing what to expect can help decrease your anxiety. It also helps to keep your expectations realistic. If you don't expect smooth sailing, you won't be surprised when storms arise. Keep in mind that the valleys, even though they don't feel good at the time, are as vital to achieving your goal as the peaks. Rather than viewing them as discouraging failures, you need to reframe them as inevitable and essential parts of the process. Why? Because without them, change cannot occur. It is from the valleys that you learn what you need to do differently in order to reach your goal.

•

We were halfway through the tour, in Melbourne, Australia at the 12,450.775-mile mark. It was a time to take stock of our accomplishments, how we'd lived and what we'd done. Back at the office, they had even taken an inventory. One year on the road. Postcards written: 1,086. Laundries done: 365. Flat tires: 63. Pairs of gloves worn out: 47. Rolls of tape used: 100. Times robbed: 4. Robberies solved: 0. Wheelchairs worn out: 1. Official receptions attended: 59. Wheelchair strokes: approximately 7,180,800. We hoped we had learned from the experience. We'd better have, because now we had to do it all over again.

The next day, I recall wheeling out of Melbourne into 30-mile-per-hour headwinds. It was rough going. Knowing I had reached the halfway point made a big difference. Otherwise, I would have really had some problems motivating myself that day. I realized that if I had wheeled that distance once, I could do it again. Every stroke was taking me one step closer to home. I remember attacking that day with extra vigour.

Hitting the halfway point was a high. However, returning to the North American continent and arriving in Miami was a major let-down. I had been on the road for almost a year and a half. It had been a year since I left the United States, but when I came back nothing much had changed. At this point, I had gone through 32 countries and across four continents and had wheeled three-quarters of the distance, yet the response was almost the same. The fund-raising efforts had produced dismal results, public awareness and media attention were not much better. It was extremely frustrating. The only thing that kept me going was that sense of "look how far I've come." That thought allowed me to overcome my emotional dip.

•

Strategy: Charting Your Change-Line

Now, let's track the movement—the peaks and valleys—toward your goal. This exercise involves two steps.

First, using a line graph like the one illustrated below, chart your objective change-line. Your objective change-line is what you do, the actions you take. This line always slants upward because as you do things to reach your goal, you are in a state of continuous movement forward. To do this, you will need to refer to the list of key components you devised in Step #3. Draw a line from the lower left-hand side of the graph to the upper right-hand side of the graph. For each key component, place an X on the line. Beside each X, place a number to reflect the component it represents. On the horizontal line labelled 'Actions,' write down the component that corresponds to each of the numbers. Use the example provided below as a guideline.

Example:

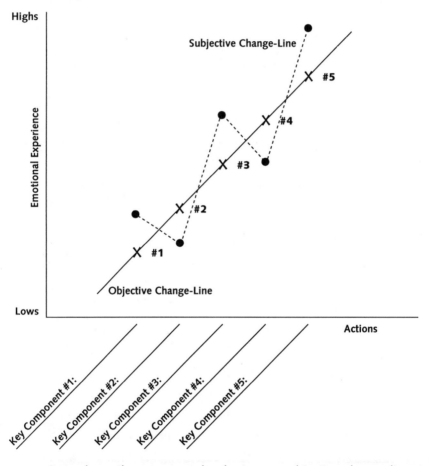

Second, on the same graph, chart your subjective change-line. Your subjective change-line is how you feel about what you have done. Using the scale on the vertical side of the graph, rate each component from high to low and mark it with a dot. Then, connect the dots and you will begin to see the pattern of ups and downs or cycles. Notice that you are moving forward in spite of the valleys you have encountered so far. By having this visual definition of your change experience, you will be better able to anticipate ups and downs and more empowered to work through them in the future.

Principle #2

Persist despite uncertainty.

This principle is a significant departure from the guidance typically offered in books on personal change. The generally accepted position is that you must believe that you are going to succeed in order to succeed. That is, you must always be optimistic about achieving a positive outcome. This attitude is held out as crucial in enabling us to persevere and to achieve success.

Yet, we have found the *opposite to be true.* We found that people who successfully achieved personal change persisted without being optimistic. They did not have faith in a positive outcome. However, *despite their uncertainty,* they persevered. Their persistence itself helped them develop an optimistic attitude, and perseverance eventually enabled them to succeed. Faith in their ability to achieve success, or optimism, came later, from their accomplishments.

Having a sense of true optimism is not merely adopting a positive attitude—it is a perspective that evolves through personal experience. It cannot be artificially manufactured from an external source. Rick discovered at the start of his trek that enduring through the next mile and the next day always brought him one step closer to his goal; he was able to create a sense of optimism from his accomplishment.

Putting this principle into practice involves persisting and persevering as you strive toward your goal despite the uncertainty of the outcome. We are not saying that you should begin with a negative attitude. We are saying that mnay of you won't feel very optimistic at the beginning.

Principle #1 in Step #4 was "Take risks despite how you feel." The message is the same as you continue to pursue your goal. Your attitude is simply not the important focus at this point. What is important is that you *act* by striving and persevering despite your uncertainty. The key is to remain focused on persisting while acknowledging your uncertainty. Through persisting, you will eventually experience success. An optimistic attitude will naturally develop as a result of persevering. Faith in your ability to achieve positive outcomes will develop and build on each success experience.

•

By the time we reached Europe, everything seemed to be unravelling. I was sick with the flu, had carbon monoxide poisoning from a leak in the exhaust of the motorhome and was still suffering from tendinitis. To date, there had been very little response to the tour. I had been on the road for months now and was extremely tired. I felt frustrated that all of our hard work was not paying off in people's responses. We were so far from home and had so far to go—it was becoming more and more lonely out there. Some countries wouldn't even let us in, we were running out of money, Tim had to leave, and the rest of the crew were running out of gas. A shining role model and leader I was not.

I was wondering just what more could go wrong: everything seemed to have hit us. My confidence was shot. I was beginning to doubt whether I could finish at all and became immersed in an all-out struggle to survive.

I could only think about each day, and every once in a while I would dare to dream about reaching Greece. If we could only reach Greece, everything would be okay. The weather had now turned dreadfully cold, and it was raining almost every day. If we could only get to Greece, it would be warmer there, and it was the end of our route through Europe—another major milestone completed and one step closer to home.

Each day brought with it another battle, but despite the uncertainty I knew that I just had to keep on struggling and focus on each day, the next moment, the next stroke. Even though I was so far from home, feeling lonely and isolated, even though Christmas was just around the corner and there didn't seem to be much to celebrate, I had to find my own personal victories in order to carry on.

So, I looked for a smile from a passerby, I searched for a wheeling stroke that felt good, I relished each hill that I crested and gave thanks for the completion of each day.

Principle #3

Reframe failure.

Failure is generally understood as an action that has not succeeded in achieving a desired outcome. Our definition of failure is different. We define failure as inaction or a failure to act, not a failure to achieve. Terry Fox aptly described it as "not having the courage to try." Ask yourself: The last time you failed, did you stop trying because you failed or did you fail because you stopped trying? Someone very smart once said that failure is the path of least persistence. We couldn't agree more.

In striving to reach your goal, you will inevitably make mistakes. Even though you will be tempted to see these mistakes as failures, they are not. Mistakes are critical learning experiences that are essential to the successful completion of a personal change. Thomas Edison had been experimenting for years to perfect the electric light bulb when a young reporter asked him if he wasn't disheartened by repeated scientific failures. "No, because I now know about 3,000 things that do not work," he said.

Baseball provides another clear and obvious example of this principle. A player is considered not just successful, but quite outstanding if he can manage three hits in 10 at-bats. Yet, he has 'failed' 70 percent of the time. Where would he be if he focused only on the seven outs? As scientists throughout history have observed, most major discoveries were not made on the first try, but rather after many tries. Let's face it, most successes, in general, are built on a multitude of 'failures'.

Now, we aren't saying that mistakes feel good or that they aren't discouraging, because this simply isn't true. But, the impact of a mistake largely depends upon your response to it. You must come to interpret your mistakes differently. Instead of seeing them as representing failure, you need to remember that they provide you with critical information about what you need to do differently in order to reach your goal. They tell you what adjustments you need to make to move forward. In effect, they provide you with essential direction that cannot be found anywhere else.

The real art of reframing is not talking yourself out of what you think, but rather turning the angle of the camera in order to see, and therefore understand, the situation from a different perspective. In this instance, you need to turn the angle of the camera in order to see the value of your mistakes.

Mistakes were plentiful during the Man In Motion World Tour. However, each mistake was considered a learning experience and utilized as such. This approach to mistake-making was one of the guiding philosophical principles —to strive for continuous improvement and work hard not to repeat the same mistakes. In the end, the tour probably would not have been completed without the benefits the mistakes provided.

•

We had sent our advance person to China to assess weather conditions. Based on the time of year and the direction of the prevailing winds, we had to decide whether we should travel Beijing to Shanghai or Shanghai to Beijing. We were told that we should wheel Beijing to Shanghai because in March there would be tailwinds from the north to help us.

Unfortunately, the cutback from 70-mile to 50-mile wheeling days in Australia had put us six weeks behind schedule. Even though we knew in January that we'd be late arriving in China, no one had checked to see if that meant a change in the weather conditions. If we'd known, we would have done the wheel the opposite way. It would have meant that we had the wind with us all the way and would have finished on a high at the Great Wall. But no, we forgot to check. So when I came out of the hotel in Beijing expecting nice tailwinds, instead I was wheeling into the teeth of headwinds up to 30 miles per hour. They would continue for the next three weeks.

A major blunder. But we learned that we had to be on top of what proved to be an ever-changing schedule. All routes, or any possible routes for that matter, had to be planned in the context of wheeling conditions and the impact on my health. For those three weeks, I leaned heavily on the strength of my commitment to see me through.

•

In addition to not trying, failure also occurs when you are not true to your guiding philosophical principles.

•

One of my guiding principles was to maintain my health, my most valuable asset. The demands the tour placed on my body, day after day, were undeniable. If I wasn't able to stay healthy, there was no way I had a chance of completing the tour, let alone making a difference. I had to listen to my body and make sure that I didn't cross the line, even though I really didn't know where the line was.

At the end of the first phase of the tour, we had scheduled a nine-day break before I would start wheeling through Europe and the United Kingdom. But I was persuaded by the organizers to sacrifice some of those days off for appearances and media contacts in order to generate more support.

So my nine days of rest became one. And on that very day, I ended up getting sick. Once again I was pressured by others and by my own expectations to continue to wheel as scheduled in order to get off to a good start in Europe and the United Kingdom. This meant that I was wheeling every day with a case of the flu. Those were three weeks I wouldn't want to repeat. I did not listen to my body and pushed myself to go on, and I got sicker and sicker.

Then, in the middle of a miserably cold rainstorm near Dover, England, I realized I could finally wheel no further. I stopped and asked my crew to take me to a hotel. I knew that I had to stay there until I had recovered. From that point on, my health once again emerged as a dominant priority. I learned to pay attention to my needs and not let myself get swayed by external pressures.

•

Strategy: Learning from Your Mistakes

When you make a mistake, you need to step back and analyze the situation. The aim is to work toward a realistic appraisal of what happened—for two reasons. The first reason is to learn from your mistake and prevent it from happening in the future. The second reason is to identify a specific course of action to deal with the problem. The following questions provide a structured way to reframe your 'failures'.

Analyze your mistake. Begin by writing it down.
- How and why did the mistake happen? Be exact and specific.
- Which part of the mistake was your responsibility?
- Is the mistake real or imagined? Are your expectations realistic? If not, how can you adjust them so that they are realistic?

- Is your mistake a violation of one of your guiding philosophical principles? If so, which one? What action can you take to resolve the conflict?

Now that you have identified the mistake and uncovered your role in what happened, you need to determine a specific course of action that will effectively address the problem. You must also determine exactly what needs to be done differently to prevent this mistake from happening again. Take time to think this through clearly, and write down your solution.

Principle #4

Overcome setbacks.

Mistakes are usually the result of errors that we make. We can strive to identify exactly what caused the error and adjust our actions accordingly. Setbacks, however, are usually due to circumstances beyond our control. But, to a great extent, the impact of a setback largely depends upon your response to it, not unlike mistakes.

In contending with setbacks, you must strive to be flexible and adaptive, and refuse to let them overwhelm you. As with mistakes, setbacks and changes in your circumstances are inevitable when you set out to make a change. Your environment is constantly changing, and therefore, to a large degree, it is not predictable. In order to cope with this reality, you need to expect the unexpected and be prepared to improvise.

In developing the skills to overcome setbacks, you are learning important life skills required to sustain all kinds of personal change. Like mistakes, setbacks need to be viewed as important parts of the change process. Each time you overcome a setback, it helps to increase your sense of confidence.

Setbacks were rampant on the Man In Motion World Tour. Rick experienced sickness and injury, crew members became ill, sponsors withdrew their support, weather was often harsh and unpredictable, and equipment failed or was stolen. Despite these setbacks, Rick and the rest of the crew persisted and persevered.

•

On tour, we were the victims of four robberies. One of them occurred as we came out of the Middle Eastern leg of the tour. We had videotaped extensively in Bahrain, Jordan and Israel and, particularly, the crossing of the Allenby Bridge, separating Jordan and Israel. On a stopover in the Los Angeles airport en route to New Zealand, Don put the video camera down near our other baggage for just a moment. When he turned around, it was gone and so was all the irreplaceable videotape of our journey through the Middle East.

And then in New Zealand, much of our custom-made clothing and equipment valued at $3,000 was stolen from our motel room. Even worse, the thieves also made off with a number of journals and audio recordings—all of little value to them, but invaluable to us. The New Zealand Herald ran a front page picture and story on the unfortunate event and the locals rallied to the cause with donations.

•

Among the most challenging setbacks Rick and his road crew faced was bad timing.

•

We were supposed to come back home to Vancouver in October 1986 for the close of EXPO 86, but because of our cutback from 70-mile to 50-mile wheeling days at the halfway point, we would be coming home in May 1987, six months later than scheduled. This meant that I would have to wheel across Canada during the dead of winter. Despite doing everything in our power to avoid this possibility, we were now faced with this worst-case scenario.

The response was negative from within the organization. The home base staff tried to persuade me to wheel instead into South America until spring and then return to Canada to complete the push. The crew was skeptical and concerned about the logistics as well as my health. There were many uncertainties. Could it be done? What about the wheelchair getting traction in the snow? With no feeling in my legs how could we guard against frostbite? How difficult would it be to grip the pushrims in the cold? What about becoming stranded during a blizzard? What about road safety and sharing the roads with cars and trucks? What about communications? Clearly, there were numerous legitimate and serious concerns about wheeling through a Canadian winter.

The timing was definitely a major setback. But, we could not let this fact discourage us from taking the route that we knew was right. We had to approach this setback like all the other ones—with the attitude that we would find the answers by breaking the setback down into its various components, minimizing the risks and striving forward despite the challenges we knew lay ahead.

So, we called on our resources, brought in experts to help us in specific areas, developed a plan of attack and, most of all, started to meet this setback with a can-do attitude. The first major challenge was to bring in an R&D team of wheelchair designers, engineers, mechanics and innovators to tackle the complex task of developing a special wheelchair that could be pushed through ice and snow. After months of planning and designing and testing, they came up with a four-wheel-drive wheelchair. It worked with chains that were attached to sprockets on the inside of the hubs of the back wheels that linked up to sprockets that were inside of the front wheels. When I pushed the rear wheels—presto!—the chain drove the front wheels, giving better traction in the snow and ice.

We were going to be wheeling in -50 degree temperatures with windchill, so it was imperative that we have quality win-

ter clothing, tailor-made for a guy wheeling in a wheelchair. They sent one of my friends into a cold room laboratory at Simon Fraser University to test the fabric's insulative properties, blowing -30 degree air on him for hours while he wheeled on stationary rollers. Frostbite was a serious potential danger— because my legs were paralyzed I couldn't feel if they were getting cold. Technologists developed a skin-temperature sensing unit that had eight sensors on each leg, from the tips of my toes to mid-thigh, with the leads all hooked up to a monitor that displayed the temperature at each location at one-minute intervals. The monitor was attached to the front of the wheelchair, so that I could easily tell if I was getting too cold. If I was, I could just take a break and warm up in the motorhome, or add more insulative material, or if all else failed we had a special army arctic survival catalytic heater that would actually blow warm air through tubes under my clothes onto my legs. Special gloves were developed to maximize the grip on the pushrims, along with de-icing spray for any build-up that developed.

There was a very real chance that we could get snowed in during a blizzard, and therefore we needed a second motorhome to house the entire crew, back-up generators, supplies for a week and satellite communications technology in case we needed to contact the outside world. In case there was an emergency, we had an all-terrain vehicle that could get a person out in any conditions. The RCMP also developed a traffic control protocol that allowed traffic to safely slow down and be escorted past us without incident.

The team effort and planning that went into preparing for this challenge were infectious. We were able to plan and prepare for any possible occurrence. Sure, there were still risks, but they were minimized, and we were so ready that by the time late November came along we actually looked forward to the winter.

•

Setbacks need to be evaluated as they occur. Some setbacks you can overcome, others you cannot. You must strive to overcome those that are surmountable and adapt to those that are insurmountable. Too often we waste valuable time and energy on things over which we have no control.

•

I had no control over the paralysis; it controlled me. However, I didn't sit back and accept my disability as a fixed condition. Sure, it was a fact that my legs were paralyzed. But, my situation was not fixed; it had borders or frontiers that I could explore and push toward, if I were not dragged down by pessimism. What I could and could not do in the future depended significantly on my own efforts. Within those limitations, I could set goals. I had to build my upper body, develop coordination and learn how things were done from the position I now occupied. Learning to use braces to stand, walking with a walker, using the wheelchair, self-care, transferring into and out of my wheelchair—there was a lot to learn.

•

Strategy: Analyzing the Setbacks

When confronted with a setback, step back and analyze the situation. As with mistakes, the aim is to work toward a realistic appraisal of the situation in order to establish a specific action plan for dealing with the problem. Here is a series of questions to guide you. Write down your answers in your journal.

- Identify the setback. How and why did it happen? Be exact and specific.
- Assess the size and intensity of the setback in relation to your goal. Be exact and specific.
- Is the setback real or imagined? Are your expectations realistic? If not, how can you adjust them so that they are realistic?
- Objectively, can you overcome the setback, or is it out of your control? Does it involve other people or aspects of your environment beyond your control? If the setback is surmountable, what

exactly do you need to do to overcome it? If the setback is insurmountable, what exactly do you need to do to adjust to it? To answer this last question, you may need to re-evaluate your goal (see Step #1) or your plan for achieving it (see Step #3).

Principle #5

Stay focused.

In order to successfully reach your goal, you need to maintain a concentrated focus. You must be prepared to put blinders on and resist distractions.

For example, if your goal is to return to college, the elements which will facilitate achieving that goal must become foreground and those that hinder it must recede into the background. Classes, labs, and especially studying, will require your dedicated time. Recreational activities and socializing will have to take a back seat. You must postpone immediate gratification in order to reap the future benefits that staying focused will bring. It's not unlike a disciplined savings program. If you are saving for a down payment on a new car, you must remain focused on that goal. Allowing yourself to become distracted by other possible purchases not only weakens your resolve, it might just prevent you from owning that new car.

Staying focused on the Man In Motion World Tour goal of wheeling round the world sometimes meant foregoing what appeared to be an incredible opportunity for personal success or even financial security. The integrity of the tour and the message were always more important than any promotional or fund-raising event. The key was commitment.

•

It wasn't long after we started the tour that we were offered an appearance on Johnny Carson's Tonight Show. Wow! We had just started and this was a big break for us. Some enter-tainers try for years to get on that show, and here it was falling into our lap. But, the condition was that they couldn't say exactly when they wanted us to appear. They said, "Look, just come to the theatre at the studio in Los Angeles, and we'll book you in." But Amanda said, "Rick, if you come back from, say, New York or Miami or Europe to do the Johnny Carson Show just for the sake of publicity, where is it all going to end? Next thing you know, you're going down to Australia for a million dollar fund-raising event. And then, you're going to come back for another media event in Canada, and on and on, and you're going to forget what this is really all about. You're going to lose your focus, and your integrity, and your principles." And, you know, she was right. . . . We never did make the Johnny Carson Show.

●

Zeroing in on the immediate task and breaking it down into bite-sized chunks also helps to sustain focus.

●

Don't look down at the road, I told myself. You might scare yourself spitless. Just wheel one session at a time, three hours and 23 miles every session, three sessions every day. Don't think about 24,901.55 miles—think about 23. Slice this thing into realistic, manageable sections or go nuts. Plug along. You want to worry about something, worry about body parts falling off.

●

Another way to maintain focus is to pick a word to centre on and then concentrate even harder.

●

Struggling up the Siskiyous summit in Oregon, I blocked the world out, concentrating on the task at hand, repeating one 'power word' over and over: "Push! . . . Push! . . . Push!" There was nothing magical or mystical about it. It was just a way of focusing on one thing so my mind could lock on totally to the job at hand. I've had people laugh and say if it's so effective, why didn't I use a more sensible power word? Like 'locomotive' or 'car'. Let 'em laugh. It worked for me then and it continues to work now. Two miles. "Push! . . ." Two more miles. "Push! . . ." Nothing else mattered but the road and the hill and beating both of them. At times I was almost overcome with the emotion of it. I was burning hot, but there were goose bumps on my arms. I didn't want rest periods, I wanted to keep going; do it all in one swoop, get it over. No hill was going to beat me. We'd worked too long and too hard, all of us. "Push! . . ." And suddenly, we were at the summit.

•

Strategy: Keeping Your Focus

If you're having trouble staying focused on your objective, go back and remind yourself of your commitment (see Step #1) and your guiding philosophy (see Step #3).

If you're having trouble maintaining focus as you tackle individual tasks, try this.

First, list the task and then break it down into bite-sized chunks. Focus on completing one chunk, then another and another. Before you know it, the whole task will be completed.

To help you focus on the completion of individual tasks, make a list of power words. You may select different power words for different tasks.

Principle #6

Utilize the help of others.

As you strive toward your goal, you need to effectively access the help of others. Remember—strength in numbers. For example, discussing a mistake or a setback with others can often lead to a new perspective on the situation. Actively seeking advice or input from others can be a way to get moving again when you are confronted with setbacks that feel overwhelming. If your goal is to be promoted, for example, and you are having trouble achieving that goal, you might ask others who have achieved a promotion how and what they did to achieve it.

Consultants, experts with recognized knowledge and experience in a given field, can often provide you with information and suggestions that can help get you back on track. Your role models and mentors can demonstrate ways of being that help you re-focus your energy and re-direct your efforts.

There will inevitably be times when you feel like giving up. The setbacks seem overwhelming and your energy wanes. This is the point at which emotional support from others can often make the difference. Asking for support can give you that extra push you need to persevere. Sometimes, just listening to others can be inspirational and provide you with that little something extra that you need to keep going. Or, you could consult other people who were able to persevere and find out what kept them going.

Work on effectively accessing and utilizing the individual and collective knowledge and skills of your team.

•

When we first started the tour, our roles were pretty general and the lines between them were very blurred. We were all doing anything and a little bit of everything to get the job done. Essentially, over the course of working and persevering toward the common goal, we had refined our roles, obligations and expectations of each other. As the complexity of the tour expanded, we had to bring in more specialized help—a logistical planner, fundraisers, marketing people, people in communications and public relations, chief operating officers, accountants and computer experts. By the time we finished, we were operating as a finely tuned machine and our team had expanded dramatically. When we began, critics labelled us 'bush league' and told us we wouldn't get anywhere. By the time we came back, we were being criticized for being too 'slick'. Sometimes, you just can't win.

•

The example below illustrates effective teamwork that evolved out of recognizing a problem and working collectively to resolve it.

•

Before I left on tour, I had a tendon problem. This injury had major implications for the tour. We had formed a medical committee made up of doctors, physiotherapists, a fitness manager and a nutritionist before we left. They had planned for every component that would affect my health, from nutrition to injury prevention, proper clothing and my weight. They also coordinated a contact list of doctors to dentists around the world who would be available on call if necessary. So, a medical team was monitoring the broader situation at home, but there was no one immediately accessible. Enter Amanda, my physiotherapist.

At first, we blundered blindly into situations and cleaned up the mess later. I would wheel, run into certain terrain or weather conditions and get injured. Amanda would do damage control. The situation required ingenuity and creativity because standard procedure with injuries is rest, and that wasn't an option. As Amanda monitored my condition, she began to recognize patterns. Certain conditions created certain injuries. Together, we developed a system to address this. We were able to avoid further injuries by making changes and adjustments in the equipment—size of the pushrim, size of the wheel, position of the seat, position of the axle and so on.

We got to the point where we would send out the advance person and, for each mile, record the elevation, road conditions and grade of the hills. This information would be transcribed by the office staff, put on computer and printed out in the form of an elevation profile printout. The printout would indicate what the day would look like. Amanda would review the printout a few days in advance, mark it into wheeling segments and rest breaks, and then the advance people would organize the events around the breaks.

Based on the prevailing winds and weather, the elevation gain or loss, the grade of the hills and the road conditions, we could predict within 10 minutes when we would arrive at any given destination. This allowed people to organize events around our arrival. Amanda would also inform Don and Lee what would be required in terms of rim changes and chair positions, and then they would make the necessary changes, often every day and sometimes two or three times a day. All of this organization and teamwork allowed me to get on top of my injury problem.

It was an amazing interplay between me, Amanda as the physiotherapist, the equipment manager, the advance person, and the staff in the home office, as well as those organizing media events.

•

Strategy: Accessing Resources

If you're having trouble resolving a mistake or setback or you feel like giving up, who could you turn to?

Are you effectively utilizing the skills and knowledge of the team you established in Step #3?

You can and should ask for help and support from others when you need it, but ultimately, you cannot depend on others to do the work for you or to actually get the job done. There is always a challenge in finding the balance between help from others and helping yourself. Remember, it's *your* goal.

●

While trying to get the Man In Motion World Tour off the ground, there came a point when I was confused, ticked off and afraid the whole project might sink well before it was launched. I recalled the words of a friend: "There's only one person who's going to get this project done, and that's you. Like it or not, you're going to have to do it. You're going to have to watch and be sure it stays streamlined. You're going to have to keep it lean and mean until it can walk, and then until it can run, and finally until it can race. If it tries to run before it can walk, there'll be nothing but chaos all the way through. There is no easy way." More prophetic words have never been uttered, at least not to me.

Summary

Step #6

Actively Striving

Principles

#1. Recognize that change is cyclic.
#2. Persist despite uncertainty.
#3. Reframe failure.
#4. Overcome setbacks.
#5. Stay focused.
#6. Utilize the help of others.

STEP #7

EXPERIENCING SUCCESS

Deni Eagland, Vancouver Sun

The last turn, wheeling up the podium and breaking through the ribbon said I was home and it was done. We'd done it! Together, we'd done it.

M ay 22, 1987. It was one of those magical moments when your dream and reality actually meet. Feelings rushed through me in waves. The thrill of having an honour guard of my wheelchair buddies pushing with me up a final hill in Port Coquitlam. Hearing Ron Minor driving me on as I'd driven myself two years ago on the slopes of the Siskiyous. "Push! . . . Push! . . . Push!" Many thousands of cheering onlookers formed a human chain on both sides of the street from the suburbs to the Pacific National Exhibition grounds.

Coming over the hill and looking down Hastings Street to the city itself—a view I'd ached for countless times in the past two years. I'd received all kinds of offers to come back for a day or two during the tour and had turned them all down on principle. It was my vision of Vancouver—how it would be on that last day of the tour—that drove me onward for two years. That one moment made it all worthwhile. The reality of that day matched my vision—now nearly a decade old— almost exactly. The crowds, the cheers, the weather, the smell of the sea breeze, the feelings, the sense of satisfaction, that indescribable sense of being on top of the world, the sheer excitement of it all. Wheeling into the heart of the city through mobs of people from every walk of life. Offices emptied and pubs cleared out. I could see and hear people leaning out windows shouting and waving, horns and sirens blasting.

Touching as many outstretched hands as I could, I rolled into the final turn of the trip, up Cambie Street to the Oakridge Shopping Mall where it had all begun two years, two months, and two days before. Tears welled as I passed a group of patients and staff members from G. F. Strong, the rehabilitation centre *where I'd learned to fight, work and force myself to push on. I remember thinking that I'd come full circle in more ways than one. Maybe some day I'd have it all sorted out. But not then, I was on a joyous sensory overload. I made the last turn into Oakridge, wheeled onto the stage and broke through the ribbon that said I was home, and it was done. I looked at the team gathered around me. We'd done it! Together, we'd done it.*

•

You've done it! Through hard work and determined perseverance, you are rewarded with the experience of success. Each step you've taken, from setting and envisioning your goal to implementing your action plan, has individually and collectively brought you to this point.

Culmination and Completion

This step will be marked by an event that signifies the culmination of your efforts and the completion of your goal. With this event comes a potent sense of accomplishment and personal fulfilment. For some, it is a peak experience.

It may involve an external event such as a formal graduation ceremony or it may involve a more internal experience such as how you feel after a business meeting in which you artfully used a new skill. The event may be planned or unexpected, and it may come some time *after* you have completed your goal. Whatever the event and however it unfolds, you immediately recognize it when it arrives. It is that moment when you feel done. You feel satiated—a thirst has finally been quenched. This moment is an important event marking the completion not only of the goal, but of the process as well.

Principle #1

Recognize that success is both objective and subjective.

The experience of success is both objective and subjective. It is objective in the sense of accomplishing what you set out to do. It is also subjective in the sense of how you feel about what you've accomplished. Or, if you didn't manage to reach your goal, what did you accomplish and how do you feel about that accomplishment? Alternatively, you can have objective success and subjective failure. For example, you can objectively achieve your goal, but it might not feel like a success if you had to violate a guiding philosophical principle to get there.

And, you can have a subjective success and objective failure. Look at the example set by Terry Fox. His Marathon of Hope project in 1980 was perceived by some as an objective failure because Terry was unable to complete his one-legged trek across Canada. However, the subjective success of his marathon is perpetuated by the awareness raised in so many people about a deadly disease.

There's no question that it is important and meaningful to achieve your goal. But, success is not only defined in terms of goal attainment. Try not to be so focused on the objective that you don't see the other successes, perhaps smaller and more subtle gains, that you achieve along the way. You only need to draw them out, to become aware of their significance.

For example, remember we defined failure as not having the courage to try. Conversely, the effort of trying can be a success in and of itself. To us, the real meaning of success is the willingness to accept the ultimate human challenge to fulfil our potential. We all have the potential to change, to grow and to move forward. The challenge is to accept that responsibility to try. By going through the process outlined in this book, whether or not you have achieved your goal, you have tried. That is truly a significant achievement.

●

Although we did experience an objective success with the tour—raising more than double the $10 million we originally set as our goal—the one thing that I wanted out of the tour, my own personal definition of success when I came back and it was all over, was to be able to wake up in the morning, look at the bedroom wall, and see a picture of me in my wheelchair, pushing along the Great Wall of China. Lying there, staring at it, I remember what it took to get there and remind myself, as I often have to—there are no walls too big to climb.

As I recall, that day was perfect for the climb. We'd hired a commercial photographer. Both the CBC and CTV networks had cameras there. The wire services were well represented. My plan of attack was simple: in places where there were stairs, the crew would have to lift me. Otherwise, no matter what the grade, all they were to do was stay behind me to grab the chair if necessary. I was going to climb this thing, not be carried.

It was unbelievably difficult. The books hadn't lied about the grade—45 to 60 degrees. After every stroke, someone had to brace the chair from behind to keep it from rolling backward; I couldn't get my hands back up to the top of the pushrims quickly enough to brake it myself. When we came to the stairs, every hundred yards, the crew carried me. The total, I'm told, was 103 steps. Otherwise, it was me and the wall, just as I'd always pictured it.

●

A particularly meaningful point of success happened on the last day when Rick witnessed the impact of the tour on one individual.

●

Eighteen-year-old Kerris Huston, badly injured in a car accident two years earlier, pushed away the hand of a would-be helper and walked unaided across the stage at Oakridge. Her voice was slurred—she was obviously nervous. But she spoke to me, and she proved again that the effort was worth the prize: "One year ago I was in a wheelchair. You showed me how to reach for the stars. You gave me that encouragement to be the best I can. I thank you for letting me share a part of your dream." Then she walked back to her chair and sat down.

•

Strategy: Assessing Your Success

Is your success objective, subjective, or both?

Setting aside your goal for a moment, in what other ways did you succeed? Write them down clearly in your journal so that you can refer to them in the future, when you're wondering whether the struggle was worth it. Remember to be creative in how you define and measure your success.

Principle #2

Take responsibility for your success.

It is not enough simply to achieve a success. You need to be emotionally ready to experience it—to recognize and accept that you caused the success to happen. To do this, you must take responsibility for succeeding and not attribute your success entirely to other people, luck or fate. If you attribute your success to someone else or to circumstances, then the success you achieve is meaningless. This is not to say that you don't give credit to those who help you; it is more a matter of ensuring that you don't give all the credit away.

Sometimes, when we achieve a goal, we mistakenly attribute the success to the help of others or we explain it as merely a run of good luck. Or, sometimes we see the result as a fluke. The point here is that we need to see *ourselves* as responsible for our success. We must see and understand our success as being the direct result of personal effort, of our ability and initiative.

•

In the last few days of the tour I found myself responding to interviewers' questions by reviewing some of the things that we should have changed, or especially what I could have done better. I seemed to be fixated on saying and feeling that the dream had not lived up to what it was supposed to be. And whenever I did think or mention the successes of the tour, I would automatically credit the team members and their incredible effort. It wasn't until one particular interview in which I had again played down my role and focused on the team that I realized that I felt a little gypped. And by myself at that.

I sat down and went over the things that I had done right and just how important my role had been in the achievement of the Man In Motion dream. I immediately began to feel better, not only about the tour, but about my part in it as well.

Of course it was impossible to overstate the importance of all those who helped make my dream possible. Without them, I simply couldn't have done it. But, it was also very important for me to sit back just with myself and give myself a pat on the back. I said to myself, "You know Rick, you did it. You said you'd do it, and you did. It's not only that you did it, but it was how you did it. You made lots of mistakes, but nevertheless, you hung in there. You followed your principles. You tried to treat people with respect and brought a sense of dignity to what you were doing, and in the end, that's all you could ask." It felt really good to do that.

•

Strategy: Taking Responsibility

Try to identify your own personal tendencies as they relate to taking responsibility for success. Most of us are inclined one way or another, taking either too much or too little responsibility. For example, you may be more than willing to take responsibility for your failures but have trouble taking responsibility for your successes. Or, vice versa. Tendencies also vary, depending upon the situation.

Identify how and in what ways your tendencies have changed as a result of going through the change process.

Principle #3

Celebrate your success.

This is the time to acknowledge your success by taking pride in your achievement and celebrating it. Celebrating your success is part of taking ownership of it and responsibility for it. Mark the event with your own private celebration. Part of celebrating is acknowledging the role that others played in your success, and celebrating it with them, too.

Success provides an important vantage point. If it goes unnoticed, you don't fully benefit from the experience. The experience of success is too often muted, so we encourage you to slow down and savour the moment. Don't rush on to the next goal. Relish the exhilarating feeling of success. Allow the energizing sense of it to become an influence in your life. Seize the moment, and punctuate it!

The experience of success has enormous potential and significance for changing and clarifying aspects of your life. Do you notice how different the world looks when you feel good? Somehow, obstacles don't look so absolute and insurmountable.

This, then, is a good time to look at life's opportunities and challenges with the heady feeling of success fresh in your mind.

•

I celebrated my success in many different and important ways. On the evening of the final day, Amanda and I celebrated with an intimate evening, just the two of us having our own private victory celebration. It was a time for me to acknowledge her role in this achievement and a time for us just to feel good about what we had accomplished together.

We also had celebrations for the team, the volunteers and the corporations. And then, of course, there was the official celebration at B.C. Place. Fifty-thousand people turned out for the welcome-home party. There were scores of musicians and dancers. My honour guard was there, the elite of Canada's wheelchair athletes, and I was so proud to be sharing the moment with them because of our common bond. They, more than anyone, understood what the tour was all about. There was a parade of nations, hundreds of disabled persons, front row centre, as honoured guests.

David Foster and John Parr were there, playing "St. Elmo's Fire," the song they had written that had become our anthem. We wheeled in a circle around the stadium, trying to show everyone how much their support had meant. The premier confirmed a grant to match the donations. He announced an additional grant of $1 million for upgrading the spinal cord unit at Shaughnessy Hospital and the formation of a premier's advisory council to give disabled persons direct access to government. It was a warm and wonderful celebration, a meaningful recognition of and commitment to the disabled of our province and our country. For me, it capped two days as perfect as I'd dreamed they'd be when I first dared to think about the finish line.

•

Strategy: Celebrating Creatively

Re-enact the success. Tell somebody who matters to you what you did. Tell the story—the tribulations and the victories—in all its detail. Engage in some healthy bragging behaviour.

Select a memento to symbolize the experience. (Remember Rick's picture of himself wheeling the Great Wall?) It may be a ribbon, a medal, a photograph, a chunk of rock from that mountain you've climbed. Any time you look at it you'll smile with recollected glory.

Attach music to your success, like the tour's anthem, "St. Elmo's Fire." In the future, when you hear that song on the radio, the warm memories of your success will come flooding back. And, if you're ever struggling and need a bit of a boost, the associations you feel when you play that song will help you through your down period.

Principle #4

Identify the ingredients of your success.

Remember, the process we have outlined in this book is merely a guide to personal change. Of necessity, each person's experience of the journey will be individualized, just as each person's destination is unique. *Therefore, achieving a success experience reveals and clarifies the unique ingredients required for your own brand of success.*

Once you have uncovered and consolidated your recipe for success, you can apply it to other goals. As you repeat the process and set new goals, you clarify and refine the recipe even further. In order to do this, you must take the time to reflect on the experience. Draw out its meaning. Make your personal recipe explicit.

•

At the end of the tour, I had an opportunity to reflect. Writing the Man In Motion book helped because it made me think about the tour and my life, and what was next. This is so important because it's easy to get caught up in the 'doing' of things and forget to sit back and think about how you did it. It's important to clarify and extract those lessons so you can continually improve yourself. So what did I learn? What worked for me?

What worked was setting the right goal and committing myself 100 percent to its completion. I learned that commitment means facing the obstacles and hanging in there, giving it my all. I learned the importance of knowing my limitations and asking for help, and of building effective teams. I learned the importance of establishing and sticking to my guiding principles. Most importantly, I learned that the possibilities are unlimited once you set your mind to something. And, lastly, I know that whatever goal you strive for will change your life.

•

Strategy: Recording Your Recipe for Success

What contributed to your achievement of success? List the main ingredients that helped. What strategies were most effective? Write them down.

What *did not* contribute to your success, what got in the way? List the main hindrances. How could these things be avoided or handled in the future? If a similar situation arises in the future, what would you do differently?

Finally, what is the 'moral of your story'? What is the deepest truth, about yourself or life in general, that you learned through your success? Write it down.

Next time you want to make a change, you can pull this recipe out and apply these ingredients to your new goal.

The Significance of Success

This step is entitled *experiencing success* rather than achieving success for a very important reason. Most self-help authors focus on the achievement of success through changing personal belief systems. They argue that if you think of yourself as successful, you will therefore become successful. But the reality seems to be that it works the other way around.

Positive thinking has its merits, but the best way to really see or think of yourself as successful is to *experience* yourself as successful. When you experience something, you feel it. It is a personal, physical, kinesthetic experience, not just a dry thought or belief. By 'experience' we mean an activity that captures the *total* essence of achieving success, not just the belief that you are successful or the mere fact of the particular success you have achieved.

It is through *experiencing* success that you develop true self-confidence, and from which genuine optimism grows. Deep, long-lasting personal change comes through experience, not through artificially altering our beliefs about our capabilities.

Experiences of success are significant in several ways. You feel a sense of accomplishment, satisfaction and personal fulfilment about starting and finishing something meaningful. In the process, you develop new skills and attain a new level of competence.

Beyond attaining your goal, experiencing success naturally enhances your sense of self-confidence or how you feel about your ability to succeed. The experience expands your conception of your capabilities. In a broader sense, you extend the boundaries of what you think is possible, thereby reducing self-imposed limits. Bolstered by your success, you may realize that you are capable of far more than you initially thought.

Increased self-confidence leads to an internal shift involving more general feelings of empowerment. These feelings serve as an anchor which holds you firm when you contemplate future goal-setting behaviour. They encourage and inspire you to form new, more challenging goals. Each success builds on the last. As you become more successful, you naturally begin to see yourself in new ways. Your self-image and sense of self-worth will be forced to change as you integrate your success experiences. One success really does breed another.

Summary

Step #7

Experiencing Success

Principles

#1. Recognize that success is both objective and subjective.
#2. Take responsibility for your success.
#3. Celebrate your success.
#4. Identify the ingredients of your success.

Remember to expect the unexpected.

TROUBLESHOOTING

It is common to encounter difficulties or problems as you enter into the process of personal change. By its very definition, it is uncharted territory. Don't become discouraged if you don't get positive results the first time you try. Keep on trying. If, however, after considerable effort and perseverance, you are not able to achieve an experience of success, it is important to understand the reason why. Once you have determined the source of difficulty you can develop a plan to resolve it. Identifying the problem and how it is getting in your way can, in itself, become a goal for change.

There are many possible pitfalls throughout the process. Here, we address the major ones and offer suggestions and solutions.

Problems Related to Goals (Step #1)

Goals can and do change. This does not mean you have failed. Sometimes, we only become clear about what we do want by first clarifying what we don't want.

- If the problem is one of wavering commitment, it may be necessary to review the personal motives behind the goal. Lack of commitment often, if not invariably, leads to a failure to achieve goals. Check to see if the motivation for your goal is misguided. If so, how and why is it misguided? What can you do to rectify the situation?
- If you get to this point and discover that the prospect of achieving the goal you have set yourself does not give you a sense of personal fulfilment or accomplishment, you may well have selected a goal that has no personal meaning for

you. You may need to re-evaluate and perhaps re-define your goal. As we stated at the beginning, the goals you set out to achieve must be based on authentic, meaningful motives.

- If you achieve your goal and doing so seems meaningless, it is not evidence of failure or incompetence on your part. This is the process at work. By going through the steps, you clarified what was not meaningful. Now, you are in a better position to determine what is meaningful and set a new goal accordingly.

- If you find yourself giving up too quickly in the face of obstacles, or you are continuously overwhelmed, it's possible that your goal needs to be re-evaluated. It may mean that your goal is unrealistic and that you need to break it down into a series of smaller, attainable goals. It may also mean taking smaller steps to reach your goal, which involves revising your plan (see Step #3). There may also be instances when you must change your goal altogether and establish a more realistic target.

- If having achieved your goal you do not feel a sense of satisfaction, then the goal may not have been challenging enough. The quality of the success experience is related to the level of challenge and the amount of effort expended. The success you achieve needs to feel like a significant accomplishment. Goals too easily achieved do not produce the same satisfaction that challenging goals do. Next time, make yourself stretch a bit more. What did the poet say? 'A man's reach should exceed his grasp, or what's a heaven for?'

- Is your experience of success empty? If so, review your goal. Check to see if your goal was personally meaningful. Then, check to see if your goal was challenging enough.

Problems Related to Vision (Step #2)

It's possible that your goal is unclear, and that is causing a hazy vision. Although we maintain that you don't have to have a crystal-clear vision of your goal in order to start, you do need to have a beginning vision, a place from which to start.

- If the picture of what you want is not clear, what can you do to clarify it? What role models, mentors or advisors could help you in this regard? What informational resources could you access to help you clarify your vision? After you have armed yourself with more information, try the visualization strategy again.

Problems Related to Plans (Step #3)

You may not have succeeded as a result of problems with the design or implementation of your plan.

- Did you violate a guiding philosophical principle?
- Was the plan realistic? For example, were the key components, the tasks or the timelines realistic?
- Was your plan specific enough?
- Did you use all the resources available to you?
- Did you adequately consider other priorities in your life?
- Were your expectations realistic?

If your answer to any of these questions is 'no', review the strategies recommended in Step #3.

Problems Related to Risks (Step #4)

For those who are unaccustomed to or uncomfortable with taking risks, this step can easily be a sticking point. Even if you are familiar with taking other types of risks, you may have trouble taking one more closely associated with personal change. Remember, even if you don't feel confident at the outset, it is crucial to take a deep breath and commit yourself to taking that first risk.

- Did something unexpected crop up? Told you so! Remember, this is normal—there are some things in our environment we just can't control or anticipate. How can you more flexibly adapt your attitude to that nasty surprise?

- Did you adequately address possible constraints in your life?
- Were there circumstances, thoughts or feelings that interfered with your taking action? How could you address those now?

Work through the strategies in Step #4 again to distinguish between what you can change and what you cannot, and to find ways to work around or through the constraints.

Problems Related to Feelings (Step #5)

The process of change often generates unfamiliar or at times unpleasant feelings as we work through it. Remember, your goal is related to personal change, so you need not be surprised if you find yourself feeling differently from how you felt before: you *are* different. Although at times it may seem cold comfort, think of these new or emergent feelings not as barriers but as part of what you are gaining by going through the change process.

- Did you adequately address possible feelings that may prevent you from reaching your goal? Did unforeseen or unanticipated feelings arise that stopped you from going forward? If so, can these feelings be addressed using the strategies offered in Step #5? If not, and you feel stuck as a result of those feelings, you may want to consider seeking the help of a trained professional therapist.

Problems Related to Striving (Step #6)

Going the distance is often a long and arduous journey. Obstacles are numerous. Distractions are many. Sometimes the goals we have set ourselves seem distant, even unattainable. Doubt in our ability to achieve our goal arises, and we feel like we're not going to make it. Look at the root word of striving—strife—and you won't be surprised that the change process sometimes feels like a battle.

- Were you unable to keep striving? Did you give up because

your goal was unrealistic or not challenging enough? If so, then you need to go back and review your goal (Step #1).

• Did you give it everything you had? Did you invest yourself 100 percent? If not, then you may need to go back and review your commitment (Step #1).

• Did you persist in the face of obstacles? Is it possible that your expectations were too high? Did you expect to have a totally smooth journey the first time out? Give yourself a break: How can you be perfect at something you have never done before?

• Did you actively seek out and utilize the help of others?

Review the principles and strategies in Step #6 to make certain that you have applied them consistently.

Problems Related to Success (Step #7)

Achieving an experience of success that matters to you sometimes takes practice. Don't be too discouraged if you are unable to achieve success the first time out. This can happen to anyone. To determine the source of the problem, you may need to go back and retrace your path throughout the process.

• Did you follow the steps closely? Did you make a sincere and focused effort? Is your goal or your definition of success realistic and attainable? Check your journal to see whether you can construct a greater sense of success from the little gains you made along the way.

• Even if you did not achieve an objective success, you may well have had a subjective success—it all depends upon your interpretation of the situation. Did you gain anything from going through the process? Did you accomplish anything? Did you learn anything? Did you do your personal best? Any of these may help you reframe a sense of subjective success, even if you did not reach your objective goal.

• What happens if you achieve success, but somehow don't feel a sense of accomplishment or personal fulfilment? How do you feel? You may want to check to see if your goal meets the criteria relating to personal meaning and challenge presented in Step #1. Are you taking personal responsibility for the success you have achieved?

Although this list of questions may seem daunting, don't let it intimidate you. If you find that you haven't done something or have not done it well enough, don't think of yourself as a 'bad person' or a failure. Nobody's perfect. The problems you do encounter should be fairly easy to overcome. It's just a matter of reviewing the steps, identifying the source of the problem and trying again.

Your success really only depends on two things. One, you have to want to change. And two, you have to be willing to do the work to get there. The challenging part is putting the principles into practice, and going the distance.

Family—people living together, supporting each other, bonded by nature, by spirit and by love— what an incredible experience.

Re-Orientation Toward Living

Going the distance changes you. Whether or not you succeed in reaching your goal from an objective standpoint, you will nonetheless be transformed. Such is the nature of all new experiences. You simply cannot go through an experience without being changed by it.

Attaining your change goal is important, but going through the change process yields the most enduring rewards. We want to emphasize the value and importance of shifting your focus from the final destination to the journey itself. The personal changes that result from experiencing the process are separate and apart from any particular success you may achieve by reaching your goal. In this final part of the book, four areas of change will be explored—self-confidence, personal meaning, personal responsibility and the significance of possibility.

The Resilience of Self-Confidence

Through achieving an experience of success, whether it is objective or subjective, you enhance your self-confidence. You feel more confident about your ability to make something happen. As your confidence about yourself grows, so does your sense of self-worth.

Empowered by your success, you are motivated to repeat the process, setting progressively more challenging goals. Each new accomplishment helps build a stronger foundation from which you can strive toward your next goal. Your outlook on life and overall sense of optimism is naturally strengthened through the cumulative effect of experiences of success.

•

I came out of the tour with an incredible sense of potency. If I could wheel around the world I could do just about anything. What an unforgettable feeling!

On December 3, 1987, International Trade Minister Pat Carney named me Commissioner-General of the Canadian Pavilion at EXPO 88 to be held in Brisbane, Australia. I accepted the position not because it was in line with my career interests—at that point, I wasn't entirely sure what those were—but because I saw it as an opportunity to put some distance between me and Canada. After the tour things had become far too hectic for me at home. The trip would let things settle down a little so that I could get some perspective. Of course, it also presented me with an exciting and interesting opportunity to learn and to represent my country again.

I had no specific skills in diplomatic affairs and no hands-on experience of running an exposition pavilion. But I knew that I could apply the lessons and principles of the Man In Motion World Tour: understand where your strengths are and work cooperatively with a team of people to help you achieve the overall objective. I knew I would have available a number of capable people from whom I could seek advice and counsel. I could learn to use my skills in the most effective way possible.

After all, I had just finished two years of intensive work representing my country as an unofficial world ambassador. In my meetings during the tour with heads of state and other important officials, I soon learned the meaning of protocol and how to interact with different cultures. An initially reluctant veteran of literally hundreds of interviews, I became quite proficient at getting my point across in short, usable statements, answers and 'sound bites'. Representing and promoting the aims and goals of the Man In Motion World Tour through various news media prepared me to speak on behalf of Canada's participation in EXPO 88.

Perhaps more importantly, I was intensely proud to be a

Canadian. I had a passion for my country and a belief in what we were doing. The bonus for me was the EXPO 88 theme—"Leisure in the age of technology": right up my alley in terms of its focus.

So, I actually slid into the role with a great deal of confidence. Yet, it was unknown territory, and there was a lot of responsibility and uncertainty. The only time I felt less-than-effective was when I immersed myself in an area where I should not have been. And I guess the lessons of the tour were there to guide me in that sense—stay out of the areas I have no business in and do my own job.

When I came back from Australia, I accepted an appointment to the University of British Columbia Disability Centre as the first incumbent of the Rick Hansen National Fellowship Programme. In that role, I was to develop and implement initiatives on a national and international level, directed toward removing barriers for people with disabilities. When I began, I had no practical experience in being a university bureaucrat, or any kind of 'crat for that matter. I had no formal experience managing people, dealing with budgets or running a large organization. And yet, I knew I had lot of general experience related to all those things as a result of the tour.

So, it was kind of like starting all over again. My experience at the end of the tour was of an ample staff, thousands of volunteers and millions of dollars' worth of resources, and here I was starting off at the university with an office that had no windows, lights that flickered and no secretary. I started from scratch and had to carve something out of nothing, just as I had for the Man In Motion World Tour.

In many ways I felt confident in what I was doing because I came back to the same principles—what worked for me on tour? How did I do it? How could I recreate it? And then slowly, from a single office and no secretary, here we are in 1994 having generated $18 million worth of initiatives, programs and buildings for people with disabilities. Where did it *come from? It came from the same attitude, the same approach that I learned from the tour.*

•

The Power of Personal Meaning

Our society is continuously changing. This fast-paced environment creates a significant level of stress for those who are seeking stability and security. Our society also tends to be highly achievement-oriented and encourages an external focus rather than an internal one. As a result, we can easily become 'out of sync' with our inner natures. We tend to look even more to the externals, such as jobs, material wealth or power, to give us the stability and security we seek.

What is personal meaning? Although the concept is difficult to define, having a sense of personal meaning is not difficult to understand. *Personal meaning is simply knowing what matters to you.* Its power is in providing an internal anchor, a centre of gravity, that is independent of other people, circumstances and society. It helps us to cope with our changing environment and to manage change more effectively. When our lives are anchored in personal meaning, we no longer fear change, nor are we incapacitated by it. Instead, we come to expect it. As changes arise, we evaluate them in the context of what is meaningful to us and incorporate them accordingly. More importantly, change becomes something we embrace and actively seek out as an opportunity for growth and development.

As you move step-by-step through the process outlined in this book, you inevitably discover or clarify what is meaningful. Meaning, like success, is highly subjective and unique for each of us. No one can define with any degree of certainty what is meaningful for another. Neither can meaning be predicted; rather it is something that unfolds and evolves during the process, out of your experience.

How exactly does personal meaning evolve? It begins

with the goal you choose. Goals, in and of themselves, are not enough to create personal meaning. Setting challenging goals based on authentic motives forms the basis of personal meaning. The more energy and effort expended, the more meaningful the accomplishment. When you engage in meaningful life activities you deepen your involvement and participation in the world. Then, as you increase your involvement, you increase your commitment. Your active participation and deepening involvement in the world helps you to shore up, define and refine your sense of what matters. In discovering what matters, you foster a sense of hope. The future begins to become a world of possibility, as your vision starts to take on more clarity.

As you clarify what is meaningful, you refine your goals. This process of refining frequently leads to the discovery of a larger purpose or ultimate goal. Your purpose then acts as a unifying force that orders and guides your future goal-setting. A sense of purpose is a broader framework for understanding and making sense of yourself in the world. It may involve discovering answers to questions such as "Who am I?" or "What am I doing here?" Sometimes in discovering your purpose, a sense of community is awakened. The focus moves from oneself to a larger cause; often this new-found sense of community involves service to others. Whatever purpose is crystallized, a focus and direction for your life is made clear, and individual goals are soon aligned with this overriding goal.

To clarify personal meaning requires that you become your own authority on what is meaningful. You learn to actively resist the undue influence of others. Becoming your own authority about what matters allows you to live with more integrity, clarity and passion. It is about finding your own voice, an essential ingredient to becoming the author of your own life story.

•

After the tour ended, I imagined I would finish off a few months of paperwork and then get back to my original focus, which was being an athlete. Get past the wind-down phase and back in the saddle again, I thought. I had sacrificed several prime years of my athletic career, and I thought the time had come to get back to it. With the summer Olympic Games in Seoul, Korea, just one year away, the timing and transition seemed natural.

It was frustrating that so many outstanding responsibilities with the tour remained; and, there was the small matter of the Legacy Fund. Also, my marriage to Amanda had been set for the fall. As time passed, I began to realize that my experiences on the tour had changed me. I was no longer the same person. Logically (perhaps naively), it made sense to go back to what I was doing before I left, but my feelings were telling me something different. I kept wondering why I was having so much trouble getting back into my wheelchair training again. I'd done the hard part—some would say the impossible—and yet here I was with all these leftover responsibilities dragging on from an original commitment I had made four or five years before. Now I was faced with trying to sort out what to do next based on what was important to me now.

By December, I realized in my heart and my mind that while sport was always going to be a part of my life, it was no longer a major focus. It was the end of one era and the beginning of a new one. Other things were more important to me now. There was the work I had started on the tour for people with disabilities, and there was my commitment to my relationship with Amanda.

Then there was the question of my career path. As I grappled with it, I realized how essential it was to link my sense of community to my career. In my travels, I had experienced great personal satisfaction in being able to give something back to my community. It was an amazing, powerful experi-

ence. There have been numerous times throughout my life when I have received tremendous support from people in a variety of ways. I recognized how it had enriched and strengthened the quality of my life. What better way to contribute than to try to enrich and change the quality of others' lives?

There were some practical realities. I had essentially volunteered for four years and had used up all my savings. Now, I had to get back in step with the real world, catch up a bit. I had to decide what I wanted to do. There were a number of possibilities, lots of buses going by, and I had to decide which one to ride. The opportunities to cash in on my fame were there from the start. I could have gone out and earned a couple of million bucks in product endorsements. Why didn't I do that? It all goes back to what matters to me. Those things were leading nowhere. They weren't connected with what I had come to know really mattered to me, and so I felt internal conflict with pursuing them. I analyzed all the opportunities that came my way and kept coming back to the same question: What's important to me?

The tour had changed me. I went from being a one-dimensional person to being multi-dimensional. Before the tour I was focused externally on sport, activities, the action of life. After my return, I realized that the achievement of external goals, no matter how big they were, was not my way to happiness. I began to focus inwardly on self-exploration and personal development as the means toward personal fulfilment. At the same time, I wanted to find a way to contribute to others' lives and to my community.

So, the right bus finally came along when I returned from EXPO 88 in 1989. I accepted the appointment to the UBC Disability Centre—for me, the right blend of community service and personal interest—something I could honestly and with integrity dedicate myself to.

•

The Rise of Personal Responsibility

Going through the process outlined in this book also teaches you about the concept of personal responsibility. What do we mean by personal responsibility? A personally responsible individual is someone who takes responsibility for achieving goals, shaping the course of his or her life, and ultimately, for attaining personal fulfilment.

How does personal responsibility evolve? It begins when you set a goal and take responsibility for charting a course of action. During the striving step, you begin to recognize that getting what you want is largely up to you. It is the result of hard work, focused effort and perseverance. As you strive, you make mistakes and learn to adjust your actions accordingly. When you finally achieve success, you realize it is the result of personal effort and your ability—not luck, fate or other people.

In developing a sense of personal responsibility you realize, with a deeper clarity and certainty, that what happens in your life is largely up to you. You realize that you have the power to influence and shape the course of your life. You also recognize that if you don't exercise this capacity, your life will instead be guided by other people, circumstances and your environment. You can act or be acted upon. With this recognition comes a stronger sense of personal potency. When you take an active role in shaping your future, you take responsibility for it.

To take personal responsibility, you need to accurately assess those areas for which you are responsible. We urge caution here. Taking *all* the responsibility or taking *none* of it are equally problematic. The key is to assess your responsibilities accurately. Taking all the responsibility can lead to disempowering experiences by wasting valuable time and energy trying to change the unchangeable. Taking too little or denying responsibility can result in the loss of new, corrective experiences, and can result in you becoming passive and stuck. The key is to strive for an exact determination of responsibility. This way, you not only experience a sense of empowerment, you uncover a direction for future action.

For example, if you consistently fail your college math exams, you could take none of the responsibility and blame your professor for making the tests too hard. Since you can't change your professor's behaviour, this leaves you no options. Or, you could take all of the responsibility by blaming yourself for being inadequate and stupid. This response could result in your avoiding future math courses, which might make your goal of graduation difficult, perhaps impossible. After you carefully and realistically review the situation, you may realize that this particular class requires more study time than your other courses, and despite that fact, you never set aside enough time to prepare for the exams. Until you examine the cause of the repeated failures—which part of it depends on you and which part on other circumstances or people—you won't be able to take steps to change the situation.

Likewise, Rick first blamed the driver of the truck for the spinal injuries he sustained in the accident. Taking this position made him feel very helpless and powerless because there was nothing he could do about the driver or what had happened. Eventually, he was able to stop blaming the driver and take responsibility for the part he played in the tragedy. He realized that it was he who had made the decision to hitchhike and accept the ride despite his instincts to the contrary. He had ignored his 'gut feelings'. Once he realized how he had in the past approached the issue of responsibility for his misfortune, he knew exactly what he would do differently in the future. By examining the situation and assessing it accurately, he was able to determine some important information about himself and a direction for his future behaviour. Taking personal responsibility for this situation gave him a greater sense of control over his life.

Taking personal responsibility helps you achieve true self-reliance. Once you become self-reliant, you stop blaming others for your lot in life. You cease expecting others to rescue you or to be responsible for your happiness. You stop believing that others are the experts on your life, and you reframe them instead as advisors and consultants, while making the important decisions yourself. You take responsibility for your own successes and failures, problems and solutions, and capabilities and limitations. You take responsibility for making decisions, attaining goals and setting your own life direction.

Self-reliance is also tempered with an ability to ask for help when you need it. Through developing self-reliance you experience a strong sense of personal empowerment.

•

Six months after the tour ended, I was married and broke. I was feeling sorry for myself and complaining to Amanda about our finances. I was frustrated and kept wondering how this could be so. "Look at me. Here I am a national hero, meeting and greeting with heads of state, and I can't even pay my bills. What's wrong with this world?" It even got to the point where I wondered why some rich guy didn't come along and put me in his will. With Amanda's help, I finally caught myself and realized that I was being absolutely ridiculous.

After all, making money was not the objective of the tour. Whose idea was that anyway? And wasn't it me who made the decision to not take any compensation from the tour? I was the one who used my savings to get the tour going and to pay for personal splurges on the road such as room service and phone calls home. I was the one who chose not to forge my career under the paternalistic and readily available wing of the Man In Motion World Tour Foundation. It was me who decided not to exploit my status as a celebrity for personal gain through corporate or product endorsements. Was it someone else's responsibility to take care of me? Leave me something in their will? Had I been building my career? Had I been saving money? If not, then who bore that responsibility?

So the reality was that I was in that position because I had faithfully followed my instincts and principles. I would not be able to get out of the situation by wishing it so, by waving some magic wand. I had to accept the responsibility for having taken the high road. It meant that I was going to have to knuckle down and carve out a career through my own efforts.

But, that didn't mean that I had to do it all by myself. I had to learn to contain my ego and not try to portray myself as a hero who knew it all. I had to remember that I had limited professional skills and that I would need a great deal of advice, education and training in order to develop a rewarding career. It would take perseverance, patience and hard work, qualities with which I was familiar.

Learning about taking responsibility was more challenging in my marriage. One day Amanda and I were arguing over whether or not we would move into my old apartment after the tour. The argument went on for some time, heated up and led to other disagreements. Soon, I found myself utilizing my automatic response to emotional discussions—I pushed the 'nuke' button and withdrew behind a wall of silence.

I realized that when things became emotional I seemed to freeze, to get stuck. I felt vulnerable. After forcing myself to talk it through with Amanda, the real source of my discomfort came clear. In the end, it seemed obvious. I had been through a great many changes over the past few years, and now I wanted some familiar anchors to help prevent me from being swept away in what felt like a huge wave of change. The thought of losing my apartment was just one more change that I did not need.

I had to take responsibility and hang in there in for that argument. I had to work toward understanding my feelings and build some trust that the two of us would be able to work it out.

I had to stop blaming Amanda for the direction that our arguments took, and begin to assume half the responsibility myself.

A couple of years ago, Amanda and I were each facing a number of personal challenges at the same time. We both felt overwhelmed at the pace of our lives and mounting responsibilities. I came home feeling frustrated from yet another jam-packed day, expecting to see my wife, arms open, there to make everything all right. Well, she wasn't. She had arrived home upset at the conclusion of her day, and was unable even to discuss mine.

I found myself being angry at her for not being there for me, even for having her own problems— problems that interfered with her being able to attend to mine. I thought that if Amanda's problems just went away, I would be happy. Then, I reminded myself that Amanda was not responsible for my happiness: I was. If I did not soon begin to 're-balance' my life by spending more time on fitness and recreation, I was not only going to bring myself down, I would be unable to support Amanda emotionally. So who's perfect? I'm still learning.

•

The Significance of Possibility

By going the distance, you have begun a process of managing and embracing change rather than merely coping with it or being its victim. By now, you will have experienced a shift in your thoughts, feelings and actions toward personal change. You now know that you can make things happen. You have cultivated an awareness of and faith in your ability to decide, to plan and to act—in other words, to take charge of your life by initiating self-directed change.

With this knowledge and experience, you can begin to actively shape your life in a way that is meaningful. Your personal vision and your capabilities have been expanded. You have opened the door and entered the unlimited world of possibility. You do this, of course, with an awareness of the fine line between shaping your life and being shaped by conditions beyond your control. Your approach toward living has been re-oriented. It is more flexible, unbounded and active. You embrace change, movement and development—essential survival strategies in a constantly changing world.

This re-orientation can also involve a motivating vision for the future, sometimes in the form of a compelling direction or purpose and sometimes in simply recognizing a future rich with possibility. With this re-orientation there is an increased capacity or vitality for living. A sense of hope is restored. In all these ways, being active in shaping your own life becomes self-motivating, its own reward.

A re-orientation may not happen the first time you go through the process, but it will if you persist and remain faithful to the fundamental principles we have presented.

•

Through the disability transformation, I realized that I was the one who was responsible for shaping my destiny. I came to realize that the barriers to involvement in a full life were not so much external as internal. What held me back was myself. When I realized this, I felt like a whole new world had opened up and the possibilities were endless. Realizing this made me feel confident in how I wanted to shape my life further. My legs no longer felt like an anchor holding me down.

All the good things in my life crystallized and I no longer discounted them by comparing them with what used to be. It had taken a redefinition of my life, acceptance of what I could not control and disciplined striving for what I could attain, but my life finally emerged with incredible force as something that was once again precious.

Through the tour, I once again recognized that it was I who created the dream, who made it a reality. The tour helped reinforce the premise that whatever I wanted to do was possible.

•

The Unending Cycle

As one cycle of change ends, another begins. Seldom does another begin immediately, but when you embark on a new goal, you'll do so with a new-found sense of confidence. After all, you're no longer just a novice.

This is not to say that change gets easier, but it does help to have been down the path before. At least now you have a sense of direction. You not only have an experience base, you have specific strategies and a framework of landmarks to guide you.

•

I was able to carry on the Man In Motion World Tour theme through my work at UBC. We continued the focus on removing the external barriers for people with disabilities. But, it wasn't until 1993 that I began to realize that there was something even more powerful, fundamentally important to me.

It was clear that sports and its academic counterpart, physical education, had been critical elements in my life. My teachers, instructors and coaches had positively influenced me in so many ways beyond athletics. They had been mentors who had given me tools for living my life. Whoever said teaching a man to fish paid life-long dividends over just giving him a fish was exactly on target. Sport had always been a vehicle for me to learn and practice important life skills.

Based on this revelation, I returned to my interest in teaching. It seemed what I had often learned in the classroom was to look for the underlying answer, not just the one that seemed obvious. As I applied that to the idea of barriers, I came to believe that internal obstacles were far more debilitating to far more people than any physical barriers. Perhaps the barriers, the literal curbs and stairs and no-elevator-buildings that I'd jousted with for so long were the metaphor and not the problem. If I pointed out to others the need to see beyond disability, then I had to incorporate that most basic premise into my personal philosophy.

The scope of the Man In Motion World Tour had transcended the boundaries of disability and had expanded into inspiring and motivating people from all walks of life. My sometimes single-minded dedication to completing the tour and fulfilling my commitment had interfered with me seeing how the tour had affected those without disabilities. About the same time I began to realize the importance of family and community, and it became increasingly important to me that I foster greater and stronger connections with others.

As a single man who focused on physical activity and the external world of 'doing', the thought of having a family never really had been much of a priority for me. That was before the tour ended. During the period of catching up to the changes that had taken place in my life, I quickly realized how important family was becoming. Amanda and I were now married and I was becoming deeply aware of just how rewarding being involved with and committed to another person could be. Many of our friends were having children, and their joy in parenting was infectious. To be able to have the privilege of bringing another human being into the world and to be an active force in his or her development became a compelling force. Family—people living together, supporting each other, bonded together by nature, by spirit and by love—what an incredible experience that would be. On March 23, 1990, our dream came true with the birth of our first daughter, Emma, followed two years later by our second daughter, Alana. Our journey into the world of family has been a special experience that has reinforced for me the importance of personal meaning when selecting change goals, and how that meaning can deepen your involvement in and sense of connectedness with the world in which you live.

I've learned many lessons about myself and human nature through being a parent. One morning as I sat in my wheelchair getting dressed for work, I learned a good one. I had been telling Emma that she could do almost anything if she would just try. As I put my braces on my legs, Emma looked with interest and said, "Dad, I know you can move your legs if you try. Just try to move them!" I obviously had not yet learned how careful you have to be when teaching.

As I began to take stock of my life after the tour, the pieces began to fall into place. As I completed one phase of commitment, pointing out and trying to eliminate the barriers that hampered people with disabilities, another began. I was bombarded with messages, testimonials and personal descriptions of just how my actions had transcended the boundaries of disability and had extended to all people. I became much more focused on the restrictive power of internal barriers for all people, not just people with disabilities. I could now see that my new interest and passion clearly lay in removing internal barriers through the development of life skills.

Realizing this, I decided that I would act on my new dream. In a sense I have come full circle. I see myself as a teacher but not in the traditional sense I trained for at university. My goal now is to teach life skills to all different kinds of people in a variety of fresh and innovative ways, drawing on my unique experiences. At the heart of this goal is a desire to help people achieve meaningful goals and teach them more effective ways to manage their lives. Along the way, I want to help people feel good about themselves, to help them see the possibilities, assist them in making good decisions and learning to accept responsibility for their lives.

So, it's the cycle starting again. Now, I am much more aligned with who I am and where I came from, as well as how I want to play out the next phase of my life. Change has happened to me and I have initiated change. My experiences have influenced and shaped who I am today, yet I am sure that I will be different five years from now. I have come to expect change and now, I look forward to it.

*Let's ensure that our children inherit an even
better world. Let us help them to understand their
individual strengths.*

Afterword

It is a difficult and, at times, harsh and unforgiving world out there, one that is changing so fast it almost exceeds our ability to keep pace. Hardly a week went by during the two years of the tour that I wasn't reminded of how very much the same people are the world over. Looking back, it's hard to believe that some of the countryside we wheeled through—where people came out to greet us with their smiles and handshakes—has since been devastated by war or disease or famine. At times, that fills me with great sadness.

Yes, the world can be dark and dismal, but it's also a world filled with great hope and great opportunity. Let's ensure that our children inherit an even better world. Let us help them to understand their individual strengths which set them apart from every other single person on the planet, and teach them how their humanity makes us all exactly the same. Let's nurture in them life skills and a life perspective that helps them meet the challenges of the world that will all too soon be theirs. Let's not wait to see if they can do a better job of it than we have. Let's show them by personal example how to live side by side with one another, by emphasizing the similarities—not the differences—between us.

It all starts with you, with me, right here, right now. If we are to make a difference in our families, our neighbourhoods and our communities, the spark must begin individually within each of us. On the other side of your front door is that brick wall of reality. It doesn't go away after you return home at night and it's still there the next morning. Every day when you go out there to challenge it, remember to ask yourself: "Can I dig a little deeper and pull out something that I never knew I had before?" And when the answer is "yes," then do the only thing you can do. Give it everything you've got, and never give up on your dreams.

INDEX

A*chille Lauro*, 78
Action, and goals, 72-73, 93-94, 112-13
Active model of human development, 4-5
Africa, 78
Alcohol, and feelings, 100
Alder, Don, 64
Algeria, 78
Attitude
  as obstacle to goal, 113
  and persistence, 117-19
Australia, 160
Avoiding feelings, 98-100
Awareness, sharpening. *See also* Feelings
  keeping a journal, 2, 17
  and personal change, 16-17, 24
  personal development line, 18
  re-orienting, 22, 171
  role models, 19-21

Bandura, Albert, 75
B.C. Place, 144
Behaviours, as obstacles to goals, 113
Blocked feelings, 98-108
British Columbia Automobile Association, 57
British Columbia Paraplegic Foundation, 51

Canadian Paraplegic Association, 20
Carney, Pat, 160
Carson, Johnny, 129
Change. *See also* Personal change
  assumptions about, 8
  as part of life, 6
  responses to, 6-7
China, 42, 43-44, 121, 140
Circumstances
  as constraints on risk-taking, 80-82
  as obstacles to goals, 113
Commitment. *See also* Persistence
  contract, 38
  to a goal, 37-40

problem troubleshooting, 151-52
Community, sense of, 163-65, 177-78
Confidence. *See* Self-confidence
Conflicts, anticipating, 54-55
Constraints, on risk-taking, 79-88
Cyclical nature of personal change, 11-12,
  114-17, 172-74
Czechoslovakia, 99

deCharms, Richard, 7
Denying feelings, 101
Disabled people
  and goal of Man In Motion World Tour, 35
  government initiatives after Man In
    Motion World Tour, 144
  and Terry Fox's Marathon of Hope, 28
Distractions, resisting, 128-30
Drugs, and feelings, 100

East Germany, 78
Empowerment, personal, 148, 168
Environment, and models of human
  development, 4-5
Europe, 118. *See also* Names of individual
  countries
EXPO 86
  and Man In Motion World Tour, 39, 40,
    51, 78
  Patrick Reid as Commissioner-General, 21
EXPO 88, 160-61, 165
External Affairs Department (Canada), 78
"External" people, 7

Failure. *See also* Mistakes; Self-esteem
  fear of, 73, 74, 75-76, 83, 113
  reframing, 119-22
Fear
  of change, 79-80
  of failure, 73, 74, 75-76, 83, 113
Feelings
  acknowledging, 76-77, 96-98

and actions, 72-73, 93-94, 111-13
overcoming emotional blocks, 98-108
problem troubleshooting, 154
and risk-taking, 74-77, 84-86
role in personal change, 13, 91-94
Flexibility, importance of, 77-79
Focus
  "focusing", as problem-solving
    technique, 103-7
  staying focused on goals, 128-30
Ford, Henry, 83
Foster, David, 144
Fox, Terry, 26, 27-28, 30, 64, 72, 111,
  139
Frick, Tim, 33, 57, 64, 91, 99-100, 101-2
Fund-raising, 96, 115

Gendlin, Eugene T., 103
G. F. Strong Rehabilitation Centre, 27,
  137
Gibson, Lee, 64
Goals. *See also* Personal change
  and action, 72-73, 93-94, 112-13
  commitment to, 37-40
  constraints on, 79-88
  establishing timelines, 60-61
  focusing on, 128-30
  and help of others, 62-64, 131-34
  identifying, 12, 27-37
  importance of, 28-29
  key components, 56, 60-61, 115-16
  obstacles, 113
  and personal meaning, 29-34
  and personal vision, 12, 43-48
  planning, 51-67
  problem troubleshooting, 151-56
  setbacks, 123-28
  success, 137-48
  tasks, 56
  types, 35
Graphs
  objective change-line, 115-16
  personal development line, 18-19
  subjective change-line, 116-17
Great Wall of China, 42, 43-44, 121, 140
Greece, 78, 79, 118

Hansen, Alana, 158, 173

Hansen, Amanda, 33, 97-98, 101-2, 129,
  132-33, 144-45, 158, 168-70, 173
Hansen, Emma, 158, 173, 174
Hansen, Rick. *See also* Man In Motion
World Tour
  accident, cause of disability, iv-vi,
    167, 171
  as athlete, 27, 32-33, 164
  and dating, 85-86
  financial problems, 168-70
  on making a difference, 177-78
  after Man In Motion World Tour, 15-16,
    22-23, 160-62, 164-65, 168-70,
    172-74
  as parent, 158, 173
  personal goals, 18-19, 30-31, 36, 37,
    174
  photographs, 26, 50, 70, 90, 110, 136,
    150, 158, 176
  and public speaking, 95-96
  as risk-taker, 81-82, 88
  role models, 19-21, 22-23
  strengths and weaknesses, 33-34
  at University of British Columbia
    Disability Centre, 161-62, 165, 172
  as university student, 83
Healthy functioning, indicators of, 8
Heraclitus, 6
Human development, models of, 4-5
Huston, Kerris, 141

IBM, 96
Identifying goals, 12, 27-37
Inactive response to change, 6
Interactive model of human development, 5
"Internal" people, 7
Italy, 78

Journal
  analyzing constraints, 86
  and guiding philosophical principles, 54
  keeping, 2, 17
  and personal vision, 47

Key components, of goal, 56, 60-61, 115-16

Legacy Fund, 164
Los Angeles, 124
Lueke, Patti, 86

Man In Motion World Tour
  beginning, 71-72, 74-75
  book about, 146
  completion, 15-16, 137-38
  distractions, 128-30
  fund-raising and sponsorship, 39-40, 51,
    59, 95-96, 115
  goal, 35
  at Great Wall of China, 42, 43-44, 121, 140
  and health of Rick Hansen, 78-79,
    121-22, 132-33
  inspired by Marathon of Hope, 27-28, 139
  philosophical principles, 53-54
  planning, 51-52, 56-59
  role of Rick Hansen, 142
  setbacks and low points, 78-79, 114-15,
    123-28
  staff revolt, 65-67
  as team effort, 63, 64, 131-33
  theme song "St. Elmo's Fire," 144
  winter conditions, 124-27
Man In Motion World Tour Foundation,
  168
Marathon of Hope, 27-28, 139
McIntosh, Bill, 39
Mentors, 62. See also Role models
Miami, 115
Middle East, 78, 124
Minor, Ron, 137
Mistakes, as learning experiences, 119-23.
  See also Failure
Moscow, 78

Nasrudin, 16-17
National Wheelchair Games, 20
Negative feelings, 91-102
New Zealand, 99, 124
Nike, 59
Numbing feelings, 100

Objective change-line, 115-16
Objective success, 139-41, 155
Obstacles, to goals, 113
Olympic Games, 32-33, 164
Oregon, 130

Pacific National Exhibition, 137
Pacific Northwest Games for the Disabled, 20
Parr, John, 144

Persistence, 117-19. See also Commitment
"Personal best," 32, 33
Personal change. See also Change; Goals
  as learned ability, 8-9
  and models of human development, 4-5
  planning for, 13, 51-67
  as process, 10-12, 114-17, 172-74
  research at UBC, viii
  results of, 13-14, 170-71
  steps, 12-13
Personal development line, 18-19
Personal meaning
  and goals, 29-34
  power of, 162-63
Personal responsibility, 166-70
Personal transformation. See Personal
  change
Philosophy
  of change, 6-7
  guiding, 52-54
Plans
  and personal change, 13, 51-67
  problem troubleshooting, 153
Point Grey Golf Club, 96
Poland, 78, 79
Port Coquitlam, 137
Positive attitude, and risk-taking, 74,
  75-76
Power words, 129, 130
Proactive response to change, 6
Proctor, Bob, 22
Public speaking, 95-96

Quitting, thinking about, 111-13

Re-orienting, 22, 171
Reactive
  model of human development, 4
  response to change, 6
Reframing failure, 119-22
Reid, Amanda. See Hansen, Amanda
Reid, Patrick, 21
Responsibility, personal. See Personal
  responsibility
Rick Hansen National Fellowship
  Programme, 161
Risk-taking
  benefits of, 73

constraints on, 80-84
and negative feelings, 74-77, 84-86
and personal change, 13
problem troubleshooting, 153-54
Robberies, on Man In Motion World Tour, 124
Roebuck, Alvah, 88
Role models, 19-21. *See also* Mentors
Rome, 78
Rotter, Julian, 7
Royal Columbian Hospital, v

Sears, Richard Warren, 87-88
Sears, Roebuck and Co., 87
Self-confidence. *See also* Feelings
  and risk-taking, 74, 75-76
  and success, 13-14, 147-48, 159
Self-directed initiation of change, 7
Self-esteem, 84-86
Self-help movement, 10
Setbacks
  as obstacles to goals, 113
  overcoming, 123-28
Shaughnessy Hospital, 144
Soviet Union, 78
Sponsorship of Man In Motion World Tour, 39-40, 51, 59
"St. Elmo's Fire," 144
Strengths, assessing, 33-34, 54-55
Striving
  active, 112-13
  and personal change, 13
  problem troubleshooting, 154-55
Stronge, Stan, 20-21
Stryker Frame, v-vi
Subjective change-line, 116-17
Subjective success, 139-41, 155
Substance abuse, and feelings, 100
Success
  celebrating, 143-45
  identifying ingredients of, 145-46
  meaning of, 139-40
  and personal change, 13-14
  problem troubleshooting, 155-56
  and self-confidence, 13-14, 147-48, 159
  taking responsibility for, 141-43
  types, 139-41, 155
Sufi tales, 16-17, 82

Tasks, as subdivisions of key components of a goal, 56
Taylor, Jim, 72
Thoughts
  and actions, 93
  as constraints on risk-taking, 82-84
"Tonight Show," 129
Transformation, personal. *See* Personal change
Tunisia, 78

Unexpected events, 77-79
University of British Columbia
  Disability Centre, 161, 164, 172
  research on personal transformation, viii
  Rick Hansen as student at, 83

Vision, personal
  and personal change, 12, 43-48
  problem troubleshooting, 153
  re-orientation of, 22, 171

Weaknesses, assessing, 33-34, 54-55
Williams Lake Hospital, v
Winter conditions, and Man In Motion World Tour, 124-27
Workaholism, and feelings, 100

Yugoslavia, 78